MAKING
BAD
TIMES
GOOD

ALSO BY ELIZABETH SKOGLUND

Safety Zones
Alfred MacDuff Is Afraid of War
Life on the Line
Burning Out for God
A Divine Blessing
It's OK to Be a Woman Again
More than Coping
Loneliness

MAKING BAD TIMES GOOD

ELIZABETH SKOGLUND

Triumph™ Books
Tarrytown, New York
THE KING'S INSTITUTE
THE CHURCH ON THE WAY

Unless otherwise noted, scriptural citations are taken from the King James Version.

Verses marked TLB are taken from *The Living Bible*, copyright © 1971 by Tyndale House Publishers, Wheaton, IL. Used by permission.

Library of Congress Cataloging-in-Publication Data
Skoglund, Elizabeth.
   Making bad times good / Elizabeth Skoglund.—1st ed.
     p. cm.
   Includes bibliographical references.
   ISBN 0-8007-3022-4
   1. Adjustment (Psychology) 2. Adjustment (Psychology)—
Religious aspects—Christianity. 3. Control (Psychology) 4. Control
(Psychology)—Religious aspects—Christianity. I. Title.
BF335.S56   1991
158'.1—dc20   91-10773
                                        CIP

Copyright © 1991 by Elizabeth Skoglund
Published by Triumph ™Books
An Imprint of Gleneida Publishing Group
Tarrytown, New York
Printed in the United States of America
First Edition

To my friend and agent,
Richard Baltzell

CONTENTS

PREFACE

A number of years ago I told a student who was intern-
ing in my counseling office about my intentions to write a
book about what works in counseling which would include something of the integration that is possible between
biblical Christianity and sound psychological principles. I
told him I would have to be older and more experienced
first. I would have to be ready.

Two years ago that former student called me on the
telephone and asked, "Do you think you're ready to write
that book yet?" His question came as a bit of a jolt. I didn't
feel that much older. I thought about his question and
decided that after eighteen years of private practice, added
onto six years of counseling high school students, perhaps
I was ready.

Making Bad Times Good shares with the reader some of
the intimacy and how-to solutions that are found in the

professional counseling office. Basic principles of living that have been proven successful by the test of years are discussed against the backdrop of examples from real-life situations.

Making Bad Times Good distills what has worked for people I have counseled on a variety of problems—children as well as adults of all ages, men as well as women. The solutions to problems are at the same time simple and profound. They can be applied within limits or with a completeness that can be life transforming. Their success in improving any individual's life depends, at least in part, on that person's willingness to change and to resolve never to stop growing.

Every once in a while a small child asks permission to move into my office. However, a counseling office is never a place in which to live. It is a place to *go out from*. It is a place of comfort and equipping.

If it is sound, psychological counseling should not be shunned by Christians, and Christianity should not be denigrated by those who offer psychological help. People are made up of body, mind, and spirit, and what helps one part of a person usually helps the whole person.

Ultimately, when we humans have done all that we can do to heal the mind or the body or the spirit, it is still God who effects the cure. Yet more often than not, God uses mortals in the process of curing. That part is what *Making Bad Times Good* is all about.

ACKNOWLEDGMENTS

Writing *Making Bad Times Good* has been a somewhat solitary experience. For that reason, support and active assistance from a few key people have been of particular importance.

My agent, Richard Baltzell, has not only provided technical assistance but also read each chapter and maintained an active interest in the book. My editor, Pat Kossmann, has provided a fine balance of encouragement and constructive criticism that has helped to produce a better book. Nancy Jillard was particularly helpful at the final stages of the editing of the book. I am grateful for both her expertise and her patience at that time.

Many thanks go to my friends Ken and Carolyn Connolly and John and Lynne Whorrall for reading chapters, discussing ideas, and praying. Additionally, my deep gratitude goes to all those who have asked about the book and then actively prayed, particularly those attending University Bible Church as well as certain individuals who have expressed an interest in continuing to receive a prayer letter.

I am uniquely grateful to Ruth Bell Graham for taking time from a demanding schedule to be interviewed and to her secretary, Evelyn Freeland, for aiding in the details of that interview. My thanks also to Beth Patton at Biola University Library.

Once again my thanks go to certain special people who pray a great deal and who also do countless practical tasks ranging from dog walking, making encouraging phone calls, and installing fans to tearing apart computer sheets and handling permissions: Karl Weiskopf, Rayne Wagner, Marilyn Pendleton, Bruce and Martha Kober, Lance Wilcox, and Geneva Phillips.

Last of all, but certainly not least, my thanks go to Robert Jones for reminding me that it was time to write this book.

It is in vain [Maurois thought] that we return to the places we have loved: we will never see them again because they were situated not in space but in time, and the man who looks for them will be no more a child or an adolescent who embellished them with his imagination.

—André Maurois in *À la Recherche de Marcel Proust* Quoted by William Shirer in *Twentieth Century Journey*

Yet, for the dream builder, no place in life is without meaning, and thus no place is ever truly lost:

The pessimist resembles a man who observes with fear and sadness that his wall calendar, from which he daily tears a sheet, grows thinner with each passing day. On the other hand, the person who attacks the problems of life actively is like a man who removes each successive leaf from his calendar and files it neatly and carefully away with its predecessors, after first having jotted down a few diary notes on the back. He can reflect with joy on all the richness set down in these notes, on all the life he has already lived to the full. What will it matter to him if he notices that he is growing old? Has he any reason to envy the young people he sees, or wax nostalgic over his own lost youth? What reasons has he to envy a young person? For the possibilities open to a young person, the future that is in store for him? "No, thank you," he will think. "Instead of possibilities, I have realities in my past, not only the reality of work done and of love loved, but of sufferings bravely suffered. These sufferings are the things of which I am most proud, though these are things which cannot inspire envy."

—Viktor E. Frankl in *The Unheard Cry for Meaning*

We are such stuff as dreams are made on . . .

—William Shakespeare in *The Tempest*

CHAPTER ONE

DREAM BLOCKERS

Last night was not a good night for sleep. We had lightning, thunder, and a rainstorm, which is somewhat unusual for California, after which the humidity immediately soared. Then, just as I was about to turn out my reading light, a car alarm went off that sounded as if it was right under my bedroom window. Usually when that happens on the street where I live, the owner recognizes his or her alarm and goes out and turns it off. Not this time. The grating sound blared into the quiet of the night for a good five minutes or more. Then it stopped abruptly, and I fell asleep.

Two hours of blissful rest went by rapidly. Then, once again the silence of the night was broken with the abrasive noise of the same car alarm. Once again it went its lengthy course and eventually stopped. In another hour the cycle repeated itself.

The real irritation came when it went off at about 4:30 A.M. Early in the night was bad enough. Like most people, I hate waking up in the early hours of the morning most of all, because at that time it is very hard to go back to sleep.

Each time, and especially at 4:30 A.M., when the car alarm went off, certain thoughts, certain tapes, started to play in my mind. It was as though someone pushed the on button of a mental tape player, leaving me to push the off button, if I wished.

What if that noise continues all night? What if I can't go back to sleep? How can anyone be so selfish? I bet the owner is sleeping peacefully somewhere, while his car alarm wakes me up. Then, the big one: *What if tomorrow is ruined, all because of a stupid car alarm?* I need not remind my reader that thoughts of *What if?* do not lead to a good night's sleep or, indeed, to any sleep at all.

This time, however, I did something different from what I would have done a few years back. No amount of anger or logic that I generated was going to affect the owner of that car alarm. I couldn't make him or her turn it off. All I could do was cut the tapes of anger and "what if," realize that the alarm would, indeed, stop in due time, and then focus away from all the disturbing thoughts. The result was that each time I awakened, I went right back to sleep. I didn't waste an extra minute on the tapes of "What if?" and "How could they?"

This morning, while I was drinking my morning coffee, I called a friend on the phone. "I need a simple, clear example on tapes," I explained, "but I can't think of one." Then I told her about my night with the car alarm. We both went silent and then said simultaneously; "That's it! The car alarm!"

A tape is a thought, fear, or memory that consumes us and only tightens its hold as we try to think our way out of it. The process of playing a tape ends up, at its worst, with our being tangled up in all kinds of loose tapes that only get more tangled as we struggle against them. Ultimately our tapes become dream blockers instead of dream builders. When my three-year-old sheltie, Horace, was a small puppy, he seemed to be drawn toward long cords. Inevitably he would get tangled up in them. One day I came home from my office to an utterly silent apartment. Now, anyone who knows Horace at all knows that it is impossible to get into my apartment without either his squeals of delight or his bark of warning. Horace is not a quiet dog.

I searched through every room and called his name. Still, no Horace. Then I noticed that the phone in my bedroom was on the floor and that the receiver and the cord were under the bed. As I got down on the floor and peered under the bed, I saw Horace. He was a frozen mass of fear, sitting upright with the telephone cord wrapped several times around his neck. He didn't move an inch or make a sound, even when he saw me. Then, as I untangled him from the cord, he nestled into my arms and shook with fear.

Horace knew when he was in danger, and so he stopped moving. That saved his life on more than one occasion. Sometimes we humans are not as smart as Horace. We play the tapes of hurtful memories of the past, the "what ifs" of the future, and the frustration of the present until the tapes tangle and threaten our emotional well-being. We keep moving and fighting and analyzing and rethinking until, at times, life itself seems hopeless.

In his book *Painting as a Pastime*, Winston Churchill comments on the words of a psychologist:

"Worry is a spasm of the emotion; the mind catches
hold of something and will not let it go." It is useless
to argue with the mind in this condition. The stronger
the will, the more futile the task. One can only gently
insinuate something else into its convulsive grasp.
And if this something else is rightly chosen, if it is
really attended by the illumination of another field of
interest, gradually, and often quite swiftly, the old
undue grip relaxes and the process of recuperation
and repair begins.

Churchill claimed that the key to what I call tape cutting
was change:

It is not enough merely to switch off the lights
which play upon the main and ordinary field of interest; a new field of interest must be illuminated. It is
no use saying to the tired "mental muscles"—if one
may coin such an expression—"I will give you a good
rest," "I will go for a long walk," or "I will lie down
and think of nothing." The mind keeps busy just the
same. If it has been weighing and measuring, it goes
on weighing and measuring. If it has been worrying,
it goes on worrying. It is only when new cells are
called into activity . . . that relief, repose, refresh-
ment are afforded.[1]

The solution for turning off old tapes is to cut and refocus, and the process must be lifelong. Old tapes are not
eradicated; they are simply controlled. At any given moment they are there again, turned on by a line of music
from the past, a whiff of perfume that reminds us of someone we used to know, or news of an alarming incident that
ignites our fears like a match lighting up dry grass.

Winston Churchill's interest in cutting tapes arose after

he left the Admiralty in 1915. He remained a member of the cabinet and of the war council; and thus, in practical terms, Churchill continued to know everything that was going on but was no longer empowered to act on that knowledge. He knew too much, could do too little, and had too much leisure in which to contemplate the "what ifs" of the nation. It was then that he discovered a great tape cutter in painting. As he capriciously stated it, he "took a joy ride in a paint box."[2] The result for Churchill was that "whatever the worries of the hour or the threats of the future, once the picture has begun to flow along, there is no room for them in the mental screen."[3]

Cutting tapes, however, does not mean that we never think about our problems. Indeed, constructive thinking is one very positive step in problem solving. In a recent interview with Ruth Bell Graham, regarding the cutting of tapes, Mrs. Graham wisely cautioned: "If I cut it [the troublesome thought] off completely and just tossed it and didn't think about it anymore, I think I'd miss learning some good lessons from the Lord." Mrs. Graham continued, "I roll it* on the Lord but at the same time I'm searching the Scriptures for comfort. . . . I'm wanting to learn what He has to teach me through the experience."

Mrs. Graham went on to talk compassionately about some of the deep hurts in life that people experience, like the pain of those left behind when a loved one commits suicide, and the need to give people time to heal after such a deep hurt. However, she spoke with balance of the need to go on once the time for healing is past, even in those situations where we may never completely be the same because of the depth of the hurt that has been inflicted. She advised, " 'Make the least of all that goes and the

* See page 175.

most of all that comes,' as the old saying goes. And keep looking forward; don't look backwards."

Balance is indeed required in dealing with emotional pain. To think and talk and work out solutions to problems is a vital part of mental health. When the constructive aspect of thinking is past, however, and a tense, frantic replaying of the same old thoughts begins, then we are simply playing old tapes for which cut and refocus remain the simplest answers.

Each of us has old, negative tapes that block dream building. Sometimes they revolve around old memories— that a parent didn't love us enough, that we failed to go to college, or that we didn't marry the right person. Unfortunately, some tapes of the past can be exacerbated even in the counseling process. The *whys* of the past and the tapes of hurt can be played and examined until the ghosts of the past and the fears of the future take on a feeling of a present reality that they do not truly possess. When this happens, progress forward is blocked.

In recent years, because of our national focus on the subject, adults who remember acts of sexual abuse or violence inflicted on them in childhood have seemed uniquely tempted and even advised by certain professionals to think that if they just look harder at the past and try to figure out why it all happened they will somehow feel better. In my opinion, they generally feel worse until they finally walk away from the past and begin to live in the present at the same time they build their dreams for the future.

To a degree, bringing out the past helps make sense of the present, but more often than not the old tapes are played without resolution. Worse still, imagined wrongs that never happened are conjured up. After all, regardless of the cause of our problems, each of us must still take life as it is now while we change the present and try to shape the future.

A young college student came back to see me for the first time since her early childhood. After we greeted each other, Sara asked me, "Do you have any idea why I am so bossy? Apart from being bossy, things are going well. But my friends get upset with me because I'm always telling them what to do."

I paused and remembered her as a little girl of five. She was tiny then, and yet behind those delicate features had been a stubbornness that had helped her survive as she protected her three-year-old sister and baby brother during their parents' drunken brawls. Bossy had been the appropriate response then. Now it was hurting her. What had worked then was destructive now.

Sara remembered some of the past. Gently I filled in the gaps. At the end of a half hour or so, she smiled and said tearfully, "I understand why. Now, how do I change?" From that time on, our counseling sessions focused on how she could change in the present. Almost her whole family is different now. They've grown individually, and consequently their relationships with each other are improved. It was good for Sara to understand the past and then to cut the past tapes. To play them again would only block the dreams of Sara's future. It was time to go on.

In dealing with memories of the past, both bad and good, the mystery writer Margaret Millar aptly compares the nature of these tapes of the past with a closet full of old clothes. She introduces the concept of choice as it relates to dealing with these memories:

The past was dead and dear, it couldn't change, it
didn't threaten. Comfortable and pleasant, like a
closet full of old clothes. You could wear some of
them when you were alone, but you didn't have to
bother with the rest, even to look at them.

Some of the clothes were ugly with sagging seams,
and evil stains, tattered, too loose or too tight. Leave
these in the closet. Bring out the yellow linen dress
and slip it over your head. See how thick the cloth
was and how well it fitted. It made you twenty again.[4]

Choice is indeed an overlooked factor in playing old
tapes. We don't have to play them. Sometimes we take out
the more painful tapes from the past and try to learn from
them, or with the positive tapes of the past, we may enjoy
savoring them. But sometimes when we play them we
don't cut off in time, and they speed out of control until
we begin to feel as though the whole past scene were
· happening all over again. The ghosts in the cemetery seem
to take form as if they were real, and it becomes difficult to
remember that they are, after all, still ghosts. It is as if
things had never changed. In the words of a Holocaust
survivor, "The memories are so strong that they can an-
nihilate the present, and that is a grave danger."[5]

In contrast, but sharing with equal force the power of
choice over memories, a friend of mine who is also a survivor of the Holocaust wrote of certain past events he has
forgotten: "I do not believe the gaps represent repressed
traumas that have to be dug up and reexamined. I believe
that one of nature's greatest gifts is our ability to forget."[6]
Joseph has chosen to go on to build his dreams; and his
life as an old man is a monument to his success in doing
just that.

Sometimes we choose to cut the tapes of the past, but
we become overly concerned with frustration regarding
the present. Discontent over living in a small house, dis-
appointment over the failure of our children in school, or
feelings of inadequacy regarding our careers: all these can
become tapes we play that choke out almost all our joy.

Like the past, the future seems to provide a particularly
fertile source for old, negative tapes. Some of us fear old
age, helplessness, poverty, and loneliness. Others of us
wonder more specifically what we will do if our spouses
die before we do or how we will handle a major illness.
Some fear death. Others simply get tangled up on the
more immediate future, like the next job promotion or the
lack of it.

The tapes of the future, like all other tapes, have the
potential to get out of control and become dream blockers.
A fear of financial ruin, for example, can become so intense that it paralyzes action. A fear of death can destroy
joy in the present. Negative tapes of "what if" can become
so intense that they block positive action. One of my patients is so afraid of cancer that the tapes of "what if" have
overwhelmed her and she refuses to allow routine lab
work to be done. She claims she'd rather not know. If she
ever does get cancer, she may find out about it too late to
cure it, and her fear will actually have helped to produce
what she fears most: death from cancer.

Whether the tapes relate to memories of the past or to
fears of the present and future, a good general principle of
living is to choose how to deal with the issues involved
and then cut the tapes and go on. Sara, the college student, needed to understand her bossiness and, above all,
to change. My patient who fears cancer would feel better

if she confronted her fear by getting proper medical care and then cut the tapes of future "what ifs."

In the words of former President Richard Nixon:

> Worrying about things you can't do anything about is a waste of time. After I ordered the attacks on the Communist-occupied sanctuaries in Cambodia in 1970, there were violent demonstrations against my action across the nation. Some of my staff members wondered aloud whether we had made the right decision. I always put a stop to that kind of Monday morning quarterbacking by saying, "Remember Lot's wife. Don't look back." In that case I was confident I had made the right decision. But whether you are right or wrong, when you worry about the past, you cannot think about the problems you face in the present and future.[7]

Your old tapes block your ability to be a dream builder.

For many, a discussion over tapes becomes confused with talking about feelings or the role of faith. To some, for example, emotions like fear, grief, anger, and depression indicate a lack of faith or are mistaken for a tape and as such are seen as something to cut off immediately, rather than as emotions that need to be expressed and allowed to run their course.

Arising from my Christian faith and greatly influenced by my contact with those who endured the Holocaust, seeing purpose and meaning in suffering has become very important to me. My experience in an operating room in recent weeks, during which I underwent major surgery, was very instructive to me in differentiating between tapes, feelings, and faith.

I have some potentially lethal allergies to medications. Under the best of circumstances, allergies are of concern when dealing with the powerful drugs used in connection with general anesthesia. In emergency surgery, which this was, the potential for problems becomes even greater. As the anesthesiologist inserted the intravenous tubes, he questioned me regarding some drugs, and I realized that he did not know about my allergies. There I was, in the operating room, with an IV in my arm ready to be used, explaining my allergies to the man who would choose what drugs to inject.

Once I had said all I could say to secure my safety, the tapes began to play. *What if he gives me the wrong drug and I stop breathing?* I had just published a book on medical ethics, and arising from that research, I thought, *What if I wake up on a respirator?* (This possibility happens to be a particular fear of mine.) At this point, because I had done all I could humanly do except jump off the operating table and leave, and because I had prayed about every step that I had taken, the thoughts that began to torment me were truly negative tapes. Nothing constructive could come from playing them. Indeed, their negative force might even have an adverse effect on how well my body handled the surgery. It was time to push the off button on my mental tape player.

What remained were not tapes but feelings and faith. The feelings were those of dread, even terror. Anyone facing being knocked out by a powerful drug and then being cut open for a good two hours or more can hardly, with any sense of reason, feel happy about it. Even Christ felt great dread and agony in the Garden of Gethsemane when He faced the inevitability of the Crucifixion. I felt as if I were walking into a dark storm, but one that I had to go through in order to come out on the other side. Certainly, because of the pain I was enduring, I had no other choice.

However, overriding all of the tapes and the dread was faith. That was my foundation. Prior to the excruciating pain that had sent me to the hospital, I had been reading Psalm 139 in *The Living Bible.* "You both precede and follow me, and place your hand of blessing on my head" stood out in my mind. "You . . . scheduled each day of my life before I began to breathe" came back to me with simple clarity. God was in this. No matter what happened to me in that operating room, God was sovereign. I would live, if that was His will. I would awake in His presence, if that was His will. The tapes were gone. The dread was there, but paramount as I went to sleep was God's presence as a personal God. I quite literally surrendered my control directly to Him. Later I awoke in the recovery room with feelings of relief that the surgery was over and the results had been positive and with a deep sense of worship to God for His greatness and praise to Him for giving me more time on this earth.

In such a situation, suggesting to me that I should have no dread would have been senseless. But it was possible, even there, to cut the unnecessary tapes of "what if." I couldn't eradicate normal feelings of fear, but I could cut the tapes, and I could make the dread bearable by my faith.

Sometimes we make things harder for ourselves by trying to walk on water. We expect to trust God and thereby feel no pain. We feel that because we believe in God we are exempt from pain. We pray and expect to get exactly

what we want. When God says No to our prayers, or
Wait, we usually say that He hasn't answered our prayers.
In my counseling office I see people who think that God
always says Yes when people pray. Now, they doubt God
because they feel He's let them down when He has said
No. They feel either that God isn't real or that God doesn't
love them anymore. Either God has failed, or they have.
It's quite a dilemma to have to choose between those two
alternatives.

Not all old tapes are negative, however. Achievements
in the past, tender moments with loved ones, and just
plain fun times are forever stored in the granaries of our
minds. They cannot be taken away; they are part of the
legacy of time. My work with teenage drug abusers in the
late sixties and early seventies, for example, represents a
time in my life that I look back on with pride. Childhood
Christmases, with the relatives and the gifts and the special foods of our Swedish celebration on Christmas Eve,
are a past memory that will forever give me joy. "Make a
memory" is good advice for those raising children. It could
be aptly changed to say "Make a tape; make a *positive*
tape."

Nevertheless, past memories and achievements, even
when they are positive, can be used in a destructive way
in the present. Once again, all tapes, negative and positive, must be controlled by the habit of cut and refocus
if dream blocking is to be avoided. It is possible to be a
hero at war and never function again in normal life because the hero continues basking in the glory of the past.
Just as bad childhood memories can destroy joy in the
present, we can take the good memories of happy child-

hood times and decide that nothing in the present can ever match them.

Past joy must be savored for what it is: past joy. It must be considered a special blessing. Then, even happy tapes must be cut at some point in order to focus on the present and the future. We can so live in the memories of the past or in dread of the future that the potential in the present is obliterated. Yet in reality today is tomorrow's past memory.

Used in the right way, however, positive old tapes can be used to help cut the negative tapes of the present. My mother was a natural-born tape cutter. She truly knew how to turn bad times into good. Rainy days were times for home-baked goods, with all their rich aromas. Sick days were times when wonderful books were brought out to read from her seemingly endless supply. When nothing was going well, she would say, in essence, "Don't worry, it will work out," or, "God will provide." And things usually did work out, in spite of all our doubts! More amazing still, when she made these simple statements, most of us believed her, even though we didn't have the slightest idea of how anything at that point in time could possibly improve.

After my recent surgery, I thought of how my mother always turned bad times into good, and I began to look for ways to do this myself. I took past tapes of how she did this, was encouraged by them, and attempted to do the same myself. Because I had had surgery in a hospital that was some distance from my home, some friends of mine had come with me and were staying in a motel by the ocean. For me, the sea itself provides tapes of calmness and enablement. So after I left the hospital, I joined my friends and spent three nights recovering by the ocean, enjoying its sounds, and smelling its salty aroma, until I was well enough to travel home.

I had a choice of tapes to play. One set included *How can I afford this? What if my patients aren't doing well? When will I feel good enough to go back to work? This is a time when I wish my family were alive again.* And so the tapes could have rolled on, with each tape yielding to a new and more disturbing one. Or, I could look at that ocean, feel its wet mist on my face, and think about the sufficiency of God who had brought me in safety to this point. I chose to play the latter tapes. It didn't just happen; I chose. Cutting the old, negative tapes was not good enough. I had to refocus, or the negative tapes would have come back. Refocusing is the key to making *Cut* and *Refocus* work.

Much of what we do with tapes is automatic. By instinct, most of us play the old tapes. We hear of an earthquake across the world, and we play an instant "what if." We remember the good old days and torture ourselves with their demise, forgetting that the good old days also had their grief.

Establishing the new pattern of Cut and Refocus in dealing with tapes means literally changing old habits and forming new ones in their place. Doing this can make the difference between heaven and hell on earth. Like all habits, old ways of dealing with tapes die slowly, and new habits are formed by repetition. For example, if we drive home from work every night by following a certain route, we must think about changing that route or we will automatically find ourselves traveling over the old pathway once again. Only by rethinking each drive home a number of times does the new become old and thus automatic. The same is true of dealing with tapes in general until, at last, the new becomes automatic, and we find ourselves controlling those tapes, bad and good, rather than being under their control. Once the new automatic is in force, our tapes are no longer dream blockers but dream builders.

Tapes do not apply only to our personal lives. They relate to our work. Writers often refer to writer's block. In my earlier days as a writer, I always dreaded getting it. It was a kind of mysterious disease peculiar to writers, made more mysterious because I wasn't sure how you got it or how you got rid of it. I have since found that writing is much more controllable than all of that.

To start a day of writing is to plunge into the unknown, with a hope that it goes well and never any certainty about how it will turn out. About twice a year, it just doesn't work. The writing goes badly, and it is best to stop. I suppose that in itself is some form of writer's block.

Usually, however, if I focus long enough on the topic, the tape starts. Ideas develop and illustrations come until the tape plays full force, interest peaks, and the topic becomes the most important thing in the world for that time. Yet all of this emotion and creativity start with an act of will to play the tape even before the writer much feels like doing it.

Perhaps because of the intensity and challenge of the tapes, I love writing days. I feel enclosed in the world of ideas in a rare, intimate communication with people I will never meet on this earth but who will, I hope, be helped by what I write. To be a writer is a rare privilege from God. To be a writer is to play tapes with a very deep and yet positive intensity.

Most work involves tape playing. As a teacher, I played

tapes of the topics I taught. If I didn't first get myself interested in these topics, in no way could I communicate them to my students. In recent years, as a counselor, I find that each hour with each patient requires my becoming involved in the tapes of his or her life, so that for that hour the patient's needs are of primary importance to me. To lose myself in the life of another is to play a tape of that person's needs. Furthermore, to give constructive help involves an intense analysis of what can be said and done to address those needs. By use of the same principle, to cut the tapes of that patient's problems once the hour's work is completed is to preserve my own ability to go on to help the next patient and eventually to leave the counseling office and continue to build my own personal dreams.

The principle of using the tape theory as a tool at work holds true even in jobs that involve mechanical skills, like fixing an airplane. We all hope that an airplane mechanic focuses on the part to be fixed rather than becoming absorbed in tapes of his or her marital problems. Indeed, the ability to handle tapes effectively is pivotal to professionalism in almost any job.

People can work indifferently, without intense involvement, but in most jobs the results of such work are unsatisfactory. We have all been victims of teachers who hate their subject matter or, worse still, dislike their students. Many of us have known of counselors who go to sleep while their patients are talking.

Tapes are also involved, if with greater subtlety, in numerous other life activities. For example, playing tapes explains our experiences of going Christmas shopping with resolve to cut down this year's expenses until we enter the first department store. Music plays and reminds

us that Christmas comes but once a year. Christmas trim-
mings in bright red and green, Christmas trees with colored balls and twinkling lights, Santa Claus surrounded
by his elves and taking orders from wide-eyed children,
people with curiously shaped bundles—all these play the
tape of Christmas in us, and we willingly abandon our
resolve to be prudent. Suddenly, nothing but Christmas
seems important. January seems far away. Only when the
bills arrive much later do we play once again the old-new
tape of *Next year I'm going to cut down.*

People who seek counseling often feel they are weak
because they have problems or, worse still, that they are
weak simply because they have sought counseling. Some
have even gone so far as to feel that for as long as they can
hold out against seeking help they are strong. To these
people, the very act of seeking help becomes an act of
weakness.

Most people I see in counseling are strong. Many of
them have just not learned how to use some basic, relatively simple tools in their lives. I once saw a woman who
had sought the help of another professional because her
marriage was falling apart and she was depressed. The
advice given to Marie was to take leave from her job, stay
home, and think through her depression.

By the time she saw me for the first time two weeks
later, she was desperate. She had been thinking about all
the depressing aspects of her life for two full weeks. She
had played tapes until she was on the edge of an emotional abyss.

"Go back to work *now*" was my first piece of advice.
"Then we'll build from there."

"I can't," she replied. "I'm too depressed."

The next day she went back to work. Two weeks later she sat in my office talking intelligently about some concrete solutions to her marital problems. "I can't believe how good I feel compared to two weeks ago," she commented. In truth, the results of counseling had not been that miraculous. Marie had simply cut her tapes and refocused. She had never been *weak*, whatever people mean when they use that term. She had learned some simple tools of mental health in the safety zone of a counseling office. She had cut the negative tapes that were blocking the fulfillment of her dreams.

A great many things that happen to people in this world just happen. Years ago a friend of mine, his wife, and their three children were hit head-on by a truck driven by a drunken driver. The whole family, with the exception of one child, was killed instantly. Nothing they could have done would have prevented that accident.

Many situations can be changed, however, more than most of us realize. Perhaps one of the greatest lessons to be learned in the safety zone of counseling is that our lives can improve. Seemingly impossible situations can change. We each have choices to make, even in the area of our emotions, and the power to choose lies within each human being.

CHAPTER TWO

DREAM BASHERS

On our last family outing before my father's death, my mother, father, and I went to the ocean late one afternoon. Equipped with beach towels and several cans of chilled soft drinks, we found a place on the sand close to the ocean. For a while my mother and I walked along the beach, picked up shells, and waded in the shallow water. Until we joined him, my father sat on the shore, alone on a beach towel, just looking out at the sea.

After his death, I remembered the scene vividly. My father had rolled up his denim pants to his knees and taken off his blue cotton shirt. As he sat, drinking in the last rays of the setting sun, the wind was blowing through his white hair. Yet his sun-tanned shoulders and face, along with his strong physique, belied his seventy-three years. The sea was his love, a feeling my mother shared and that they both passed on to me early in my life. It was appropriate that this beach would be our last real place on earth together.

It was sunset and the sun was low on the horizon. Its bright orange rays dipped through the distant line between ocean and sky, while within a few feet of where we were sitting the waves came in gently toward us and then retreated, leaving behind a glassy sheet of sand covered by an abundance of white foam.

My mother and I joined my father, and the three of us sat silently watching the tide, coming in and out with almost hypnotic force, and the foam, which by now had spread out like soapsuds across most of the beach. Distracted for a moment from the scene, I turned to my father to show him a shell with an interesting formation. Then within seconds the tranquil scene was shattered by a series of stronger waves that covered us and our things with seawater and sand. We scrambled to our feet, retrieved purses and shoes, and concentrated on escaping further drenching. We moved farther up the beach. Ordinary life had returned.

Life has its built-in disappointments, some of them as small as the fluctuating tide of the sea and some as monumental as a terminal illness. Whether the disturbance comes from nature or from another human being, sometimes life, like the ocean tide, interrupts our lives in an unavoidable way. Not long ago I walked into my office waiting room in time to hear howls of rage from a small boy who had just built a very high tower out of blocks, only to have it kicked into oblivion by his older sister. The young dream builder had just had his dream cut down by a dream basher in a way reminiscent of Lucy in Charles

Schulz's cartoons when she says, "Can't you ever do anything right, Charlie Brown?"

On the level of the trivial, the disturbance may be relatively minor. Some days are just too hot, or too cold. For most of us, just when we think we are caught up on bills or have our home in shape, an unexpected expense arises or the paint begins to peel. Our youngest son, who we hoped would be a star basketball player like his father, turns out to be interested in water-skiing. Real estate soars just when we go to buy a house; when we find that perfect mother-of-the-bride outfit, we discover that the store is out of our size.

Certain big issues, too, like the inevitability of death or the certainty of earthquakes in California, are unavoidable. Although we can try to drive carefully to avoid a car accident, and take all possible precautions, sometimes a drunken driver may cross over the center line and leave us no chance at all to avoid a collision.

The examples of unavoidable unpleasantness or even disaster are many. What I learn in my counseling office, however, is that many people do not distinguish between the unavoidable problems of life and those situations that are very avoidable for them as individuals. In addition to the problems of a low self-image, the most common characteristic of people who seek professional counseling seems to be the feeling that they have somehow lost control of their lives. People may feel so overextended, so dominated by others' opinions, or so enslaved by their own negative emotions that they truly feel that control of their lives is no longer theirs.

Building upon a foundation of good self-esteem, dream building is facilitated by the act of declaring. To declare is to state one's boundaries. It does *not* mean arguing, debating, convincing, attacking, or pleading for permission. One declares oneself, not someone else. "I am going to bed at ten" does not mean that someone else must go to bed at the same time. "I go to church every Sunday" does not mean telling everyone else that they must do the same.

Declaring sounds almost simplistic. For those who have spent their lives hoping that if they could just change the world around them their own world could calm down, the technique is difficult to acquire but lifesaving in its potential. A woman I had not seen in several years called me and said, "Life around me has been worse since I last saw you. But I'm better now than I've ever been. What made the difference was when you said: 'You can't wait for the world around you to change, even if they are the ones who need to. You must change.' I've done that," she said, "and that has made all the difference."

Declaring preserves the ability to do what we have been placed on this earth to do. It results in clearing away the unwarranted demands of others that keep us from our task. It often involves saying no to what is good in order to do what is better. Declaring is not selfish; it is self-preserving. Declaring means stating God-given boundaries.

Every human being is placed on this earth for a specific purpose. If we are to fulfill that purpose, we cannot afford to go off on every tangent that comes along, just because we can't say no. Indeed, we could reason that we have an obligation to focus on our God-given course and not allow ourselves to be distracted from that course, even by an activity that is in itself worthwhile.

A psychiatrist of some note once related an incident that occurred when he was a resident in training. He was assigned to a number of patients in a hospital psychiatric ward. One man on the floor had been totally unreachable, and previous residents had given up on him. This history only spurred on my friend. He decided that he would reach this man above all others.

Day after day he increased his therapy time with his patient. Soon he spent his lunchtime with the man and then dinner. Then he came back after hours. Even though he had a wife and children at home, he ended up spending eight to nine hours daily, apart from his normal hours, with this man. He reached the point where he felt as if the man and he were imprisoned in a box, and he was trying now to cure the man so that he himself could also get out of the box. His comment to me was, "I became as crazy as he was."

He had lost control over his life, not out of selfishness or greed, but because he had tried too hard to help this other human being. The solution for my friend was not to try to cure the man so that he himself could get free but, rather, to jump out of the box himself and then declare the boundaries within which he as a healthy person could help this other person toward mental health.

There are basically two kinds of people in this world: dream builders and dream bashers. Sometimes we are a little of each, but most of us tend to be more one than the other. Dream bashing is the enemy of dream building. The weapon against dream bashing is declaring.

From early in life all of us have known dream bashers; for dream bashing starts in childhood, usually in ways that seem small to an adult but are heartbreaking to a child. I have always been fond of animals and have rarely been without a cat and a dog. My first dog, Jack, a huge Saint Bernard–collie combination, was my constant companion and playmate from the time I was about four years old. One day when Jack and I were playing in the backyard, he spontaneously licked my arm. The incident was of no importance. Jack often licked me. On this occasion, however, my playmate, who was several years older than I and perhaps was practicing that wisdom on me, said, "He's not doing that because he loves you; he just likes the salt on your skin."

That is the first vivid incident of dream bashing that I remember, and its irritating memory has followed me through life. On some half-conscious level, many times when my current dog, Horace, jumps up and kisses me, I think, "Remember, this isn't love; he just likes the salt on your skin." Dream bashers make their imprint!

Last week I was watching a video portrayal of Mark Twain's *Life on the Mississippi*. As I watched it, I realized how much my present enjoyment was enhanced by a former college professor of mine. Leon Howard was a Guggenheim scholar and a well-known authority in several areas of American literature, but to me he was much more than that. To me he was a dream builder, for he taught me to understand and love literature in the same way that another scholar-professor, James Emerson Phillips, taught me to understand and love Shakespeare.

I don't even remember the names of most of my college professors, but every now and then I had a dream builder, and I remember those names. James Bouey shared his fascination with the biology of living creatures. Ellis Levine didn't just teach me German; he taught me confidence as well. There were others, like the professor who made me write a thousand-word essay on Humpty-Dumpty and perhaps in so doing gave me my first surge of confidence toward writing.

Not too many college professors stand out in my memory as dream builders. Most were in the middle, not terribly inspiring and yet not dream bashers either. Then there were a few real dream bashers. It was the dream builders, however, who left a positive imprint on the lives of their students that far exceeded the scope of the immediate classroom. Long after we left those classrooms, many of us continued to learn and grow in the directions in which these professors had started us.

Actually kicking over someone's sand castle isn't necessary to be a dream basher. Dream bashing can be subtle. To a student who brings home his first set of good grades, a dream-bashing statement says, "That's wonderful. I'm proud of you. But it's too bad you had to wait until tenth grade to do it." For the young bride who's learning to cook, a dream-bashing compliment would be "This is great! It's the first dinner I've really enjoyed." Everyone who's ever dieted can relate to the dream-bashing quality of, "That's a beautiful new dress. It doesn't make you look so heavy."

In addition to fending off the dream bashers in our lives, it is important for each of us not to become our own personal dream basher by denigrating our own worth. "I can't do anything right," for example, is a personal dream-bashing attitude. Some people are actually better dream builders for other people than they are for themselves. They point out positive things in the lives of others, while at the same time they feel that they themselves have no worth at all.

Most of us intuitively recognize the difference between a dream basher and a dream builder. If our self-esteem is at all sturdy, we avoid the former and gravitate toward the latter. A young man had failed to be accepted into a specialized training program because he failed the English test that was given prior to acceptance. One high school English teacher stood out in his mind as someone he could approach for advice.

"I never studied in high school," he explained to her when he went back and visited. The school day was over, and the two were chatting together in the empty classroom. The teacher asked Ben what the test had involved. It turned out to be based on a few simple concepts of grammar.

"I don't think I can ever catch up enough to pass the test," Ben continued, doing a simple version of dream bashing on himself.

The teacher, who had been a dream builder in the lives of many of her students, challenged Ben. "Give me one hour of your undivided attention, and I am sure you will go back and pass the test with flying colors." If the teacher had been a dream basher instead of a dream builder, she might have chided Ben for not studying in the past. Instead, she saw the potential for the future. She fulfilled the old maxim: "He has the right to criticize who has the heart to help."

Ben spent the next hour learning what he had never really learned before. Now he, too, had a dream, and learning English grammar had become part of fulfilling that dream. A few weeks later Ben passed his exam and entered his training program.

A person who lives an undeclared life is likely to be angry, frustrated, and ultimately burned-out. To be undeclared is to feel that you can never say no. To be undeclared means yielding your own priorities to those that other people set for you. Rather than basing decisions on what is right for your life at any given time, to live undeclared is to let go of the control of your life—not to God where it belongs, but to people to whom you cannot say no. It becomes a matter of "I can't say no," rather than "I believe this is the right course for my life."

The best example I have ever heard that defines *declaring* came through word of mouth to me and relates to the wife of the late General Douglas MacArthur. According to the story, people had been after her throughout her adult life to share stories, facts, and anecdotes about the general. Her answer remained the same: "When I married the general, he was already a four-star general. I determined then that I would not grant interviews, make speeches, or write books. That has held me in good stead for all these years, and I intend to stand by that decision." The statement doesn't explain; it doesn't ask permission. It closes the door, ever so politely but firmly. It allows no room for debate. A person would have to be pretty pushy to try that door twice. It is a declaration.

Some people I see in counseling sessions avoid confronting frustrating situations in their lives by saying, "It's okay. I can handle it if it doesn't get too bad." Usually they mean that it's harder to declare to that adult son, who lives in their home and wakes them up at two in the morning with his radio, than it is to endure the discomfort. If they declare to the spouse, who makes fun of them at parties or always complains about their way of dealing with money but will never sit down and talk about it, they feel then that somehow the situation will become even more intolerable. And so they continue on, silently, bitterly. They fight periodically, but they never declare.

One day, probably arising out of desperation combined with reading too many Agatha Christie mystery books, I turned to such a person and asked, "Knowing that small amounts of arsenic will not kill you but will just gradually make you sick, would you accept your weekly cup of tea or coffee in this office if you knew that it contained ever so small an amount of arsenic?"

"Of course not," my patient answered with some vehemence.

"Yet every day of your life you go to work and accept numerous small doses of emotional arsenic," I replied. John saw my point. Since then he has learned to declare.

John is a painter who shares a small business with a partner who sometimes tries to take advantage of him. In the past, John just endured or occasionally lost his temper and yelled. Now, when his partner says, "John, I'm just too hot; you finish the rest of this," John declares his own boundaries. "I'm sorry you're uncomfortable, Bill," he replies. "But I haven't got time to help you. You're on your own." Then he walks away, without debate, back to his own task. Bill can either continue painting or face the consequences of an angry customer and, eventually, if his behavior continues, the loss of a partnership.

The emotional results of John's declaring have been that John himself is no longer angry. He has even begun to like his partner once again. Bill has become more responsible, and his respect for John has returned to what it was before they almost ruined their relationship with their business partnership. Their mutual business dream was almost ruined by Bill's irresponsibility and John's unwillingness to declare.

Notice too, that John did not tell Bill what he had to do. He just told him what he, John, would and would not do. He declared his own boundaries and by so doing placed Bill's responsibility for Bill back where it belonged: with Bill.

Simple as declaring is, and life transforming as it can be, its very simplicity can be deceiving. Many people think that such a simple concept cannot possibly work. Others think they understand the concept but don't. They think they are declaring, but they are not; then they are discouraged when what they have done doesn't work. There are several behaviors that may seem to be declarative but have nothing to do with declaring.

Declaring does not mean attacking. In the case of the two painters, telling Bill that he was a lazy bum or ordering him to go back to his painting would not have been declaring. The result, too, would have been the opposite of declaring, for Bill would have been angry, at best, or perhaps rebellious enough to quit. In return, John, who knew that his position was usually the fair one, would have been enraged. Declaring cuts anger; it does not cultivate anger. Declaring that builds anger rather than deflecting it is not true declaring.

A teenager with whom I have been working came in last week and said, "Aunt Sally was over for dinner and heard me tell a friend to shut up. When my aunt criticized me for using that term, I declared. I told her that, in view of what my friend had said, I didn't have a problem with my response. My aunt got angry at me and my mother grounded me. Declaring didn't work," she concluded. "It just made everyone angry at me."

For a moment I wondered if this was an exception to the guarantee that declaring reduces anger. Then, on impulse, I said, "Show me how you spoke to your aunt. Do it all over again, just as if I were your aunt."

Susan is dramatic, so I got the full impact. She came at me with her eyes blazing, established eye contact from just a few inches away, and screamed into my face, "I don't have a problem with what I said. She deserved it." Then, as if daring her aunt to disagree with her, she concluded by shouting, "Do you have a problem with that?"

She could have said, in a calm tone of voice, "After what my friend said to me, I don't feel bad about saying what I did." These words are somewhat better chosen. But actually her choice of words was not the major problem in her declaration. The menacing body movements and the angry, elevated voice constituted an attack, regardless of the choice of words.

Debating, too, is not declaring. "Why do you always have to interfere?" or "I wish you would try to understand me" could be opening statements for an argument between two people like Susan and her aunt. But they are not declarations.

Sometimes explanations and even debate are important in communication, but when someone like John the painter knows that what he feels is fair in a given situation, he doesn't need to debate or explain. To debate or to explain, when a declaration is more appropriate, arises from either ignorance of how to declare or from a need for the other person's approval.

In a related way, asking permission is another form of communication that fails to declare. You ask permission to borrow a hammer from your neighbor. You do not ask permission to get your own hammer back. You say nicely, but firmly, "I need the hammer returned by Saturday morning." Because it is not an attack or a demand, declaring can always be polite. It is always a reasonable statement of an individual's own boundaries.

For the Christian, declaring includes an added dimension of taking control of one's life in order to be under God's control. We cannot truly be under the control of God if that control belongs to other people. In its truest sense, declaring means stating God's boundaries for us. We are not our own, but we are bought with a price. As such, we belong under God's authority.

For the Christian, "Who controls my life?" is a major question. We can choose, even by default, to let others control us at whim. We can choose to take that control ourselves. Or we can transcend even that phase, choose to give the control of our lives to Jesus Christ, and then, under His direction, declare our boundaries to those with whom we deal.

A young woman I met after speaking at a church told me that she walked into her living room one afternoon and saw her husband sitting on the living room floor with his eyes closed and hands folded and chanting, "Me! Me! Me!" over and over again.

When she asked him why he did it, he said it made him feel good.

Taking control, if that's what he was doing, is not

enough. For the Christian it means relinquishing that control back to God Himself. To do this is the opposite of the
thinking of what has often been called the "me generation." To do this is the only way to truly find oneself.

The last stanza of an old hymn by George Matheson
stands out in contrast to chanting "Me! Me! Me!" and is
paradoxical in its truth.

> My will is not my own
>   Till thou hast made it Thine;
> If it would reach a monarch's throne
>   It must its crown resign;
> It only stands unbent
>   Amid the clashing strife,
> When on Thy bosom it has leant,
>   And found in Thee its life.[1]

To be under the authority of God and to live within His
predescribed boundaries for our lives demand the opposite of passivity. They demand active declaring. Such confrontation, however, can still be gracious. An attractive
Englishman began a conversation with me in a hotel lobby.
The conversation ended with an invitation to spend the
night in his room. I knew nothing about the man except
that he had a wife and child in England and was looking
forward to seeing them the next day. Indeed, he had
talked about little else. Seizing upon that, I replied,
"Wouldn't you feel better with your wife tomorrow if we
just had another cup of coffee and went our separate
ways?" He agreed, with almost a sense of relief. Yet the
declaration had not been an attack. It had been a simple
statement of my God-directed boundaries.

There are times when such a proposition needs to be rebuffed more abrasively, yet many times we can make our points most effectively with politeness and grace. Good manners should characterize those who call themselves Christians.

Politeness, or a commitment to "nice," can sometimes become distorted into a way to avoid declaring. Being nice to a child lying on the sidewalk screaming for candy is hardly a solution. Walking away is.

In the same way the husband who sat down for dinner, saw that it was not to his liking, picked up the plate, and emptied it into the sink should not be rewarded with a new dinner. Peter's wife, who had been behaving as the loving spouse who catered to these tantrums, ended up in my office after enduring screaming fights and unreasonable demands. The marriage was almost destroyed, and the children were developing their own behavioral problems. Then she declared.

The next night after his wife saw me, Peter decided that his dinner wasn't hot enough, and so he dumped it in the sink. Quietly Martha told him that she was sorry he wasn't enjoying dinner and that there was more food in the refrigerator if he cared to prepare something else. When he ordered her to cook something else for him, she said she couldn't because she and the children were busy eating their dinners. Then she began to ask her children about their day. A few minutes later, to her amazement, Peter stomped back into the kitchen and made a cheese sandwich. Other problems in their marriage had to be worked out, but the tantrums over meals stopped.

In the context of this example, it is important to realize that even though declaring often changes the behavior of the person declared to, as in Peter's case, it doesn't always happen, and it can never be the purpose of declaring. Declaring is to declare oneself, one's own boundaries, not those of someone else.

Martha had a difficult time declaring, because it didn't seem nice; yet she found that screaming and yelling and tantrums aren't so nice either. "Nice" is not the same as godly. "Nice" can be a way you behave because you are too gutless to say No. A commitment to niceness can make you say Yes to every demand and whim that comes along, so that you have no time or strength left to do what God really wants you to do. The end result of a commitment to niceness is burnout and anger. The culmination of a commitment to the will of God is peace.

We all know people who do good deeds because they can't say no. They bring dinners to the church but never cook for their own families. They read to the blind but never to their own three-year-old children. Such people have lost control of their lives through a commitment to niceness rather than a commitment to the will of God. They have not learned that liberation can come through declaring.

To declare one's own boundaries, to take control of one's own life without having to change anyone else, is to experience freedom from bondage. When I was a high school teacher, I spent the first two years of my public school teaching trying to get my classes under control so that I could relax and go on. But it didn't work out that way. I couldn't force my students not to cheat. I couldn't make them study. I couldn't insist that they like English literature.

During my third year I discovered that, although I

couldn't force change, I could declare my boundaries. When I said, "Don't you ever cheat in my classroom," I was daring them to cheat. Then I said, "I can't stop you from cheating, and I'm not even going to try. But if I do find that you have cheated, you will get two F's for that paper rather than the one you would have gotten by simply failing." The situation stopped being me against them, and there seemed to be less of a problem with cheating. The same became true in other areas, like classroom behavior. I didn't wait for them to change. I changed.

Declaration takes practice. We all operate automatically in certain ways in our lives. Some of us automatically shout, become silent, debate, give in, or become nasty or nice. These automatic responses are like habits that have become part of our behavior over the years. Our friends are familiar with our sets of automatic responses, and they can sometimes guess how we will behave. I hear statements like, "John always becomes quiet in a crowd" and "I just know that Susan will scream at me when I cancel dinner." These statements are frequently based on the knowledge people have of our automatic responses.

For most people, to declare means not only to learn how it works in a practical way and to develop the art of declaring by trial and error but also to repeat the declaring enough times so that it becomes automatic in their lives. It means developing a new habit pattern.

Margaret, the head nurse in a high-stress medical setting, consulted me because she was committed to being nice and consequently could never confront anyone. Particularly troublesome to her was an abrasive supervisor who was her immediate superior and who was highly critical.

In our counseling sessions Margaret and I worked hard at developing her declaring skills. Her leadership qualities grew. She began to declare well, and yet she remained compassionate and open to change. Her co-workers respected her because they knew that if she had a complaint about one of them she would confront them constructively and privately. Yet every time the supervisor came by, at least a part of Margaret's day went down in defeat. Declaring was still not automatic in Margaret's life and certainly not automatic with her superior.

One afternoon Margaret came to her counseling session radiant with enthusiasm. "I did it," she exclaimed as she sat down. "I declared to my supervisor without even thinking about what I was doing. It was automatic for the first time. I told her that I couldn't follow her orders unless she made sure I got those orders. I couldn't be blamed for not reading her mind. It all ended up a little strangely," Margaret added. "My supervisor just said that she would be sure to write the orders down early in the day, thanked me, and walked out. She was *less* angry than when I've said nothing!" Margaret had discovered the power of declaring, and for her the habit had become automatic.

Those we love and those in authority are probably the most difficult to declare to. After all, with them we have the most to lose. Mothers seem to be uniquely difficult to declare to because of the deep emotional bonds and because they are usually in positions of major influence in our lives. Yet, without the ability to declare to parents, husbands and wives, bosses at work, and other such authority figures, we never quite grow up. Declaring is one means by which we grow up and claim our adulthood, not defensively as an adolescent but with the maturity that comes with issuing a statement that simply delineates one's own boundaries without requiring change from anyone else.

Charlene found herself getting upset after most phone calls with her mother. Her mother managed to make her feel guilty because they didn't see each other enough or because her mother felt that Charlene was spending too much time with her friends instead of with her mother. They disagreed, too, over the grandchildren and how they were being raised. "You know, dear, that son of yours is not going to amount to anything if you always say yes to him," the mother finally said. Charlene dissolved into tears.

When I talked to Charlene, I urged her to declare and save the relationship with her mother before they had a real fight and said things they would both always regret. With agony, she made the attempt. The next time her mother complained about her ten-year-old grandson, Charlene said, "I'm so glad that you're concerned, and I value your prayers, but we have to raise Jeff as we see fit."

Her mother replied, "Now dear, don't get upset. I'm just trying to help." In a statement that defused the whole debate, Charlene then answered, "I'm glad, but let's not talk about it anymore."

Charlene had declared her boundaries. The mother was a bit upset, but she soon got over it. For the first time in a long while, by the time the conversation ended, they had talked about other subjects, and both felt better. The mother was relieved of the obligation to keep making sure her daughter did the right thing, a habit that went back to Charlene's childhood. Charlene felt an adult relationship with her mother for the first time.

Her mother still advised at times, for old habits die

slowly. But, now that advice at times was valued. After all, she did have insight from the experience of raising her own children. The mother gained status as a valued advisor, now that her daughter knew that she could always declare when she didn't agree.

Charlene would have to build her declaring into an automatic response by the process of repetition. Especially with her mother, she would have to redeclare her adult role from time to time. Rather than fighting back as a child, she would have to continue to choose to build an adult relationship with her mother.

The concept of choice is biblically based. Choosing God's way is the ultimate possibility of personal declaration. We belong to Him already by the right of Creation as well as Redemption. But God is a gentleman. He lets us choose. In the Old Testament, Joshua presented that choice very articulately. To his challenge to the people, " . . . Decide today whom you will obey," Joshua's own answer was: "But as for me and my family, we will serve the Lord" (Josh. 24:15 TLB).

A plaque, made in the mid-nineteenth century in Sweden and given to my maternal grandparents for their wedding, states Joshua's personal response in Swedish and hangs in my living room as a declaration of the choice of my family. It is a declaration of this household and those from it who have gone on before.

To declare is an important tool to be learned in the safety zone of the counseling relationship. It is a tool that helps to enable the building of bigger dreams than we ever thought possible. It helps to make dream builders of dream bashers, and it protects dream builders from dream bashers. Above all, it helps us choose God's way and clear

away the debris of indecision and fearfulness with re-
newed conviction and determination.

The result? C. S. Lewis describes that as well as anyone
I've read:

> Imagine yourself as a living house. God comes in to
> rebuild that house. At first, perhaps, you can under-
> stand what he is doing. He is getting the drains right
> and stopping the leaks in the roof and so on: you
> knew that those jobs needed doing and so you are
> not surprised. But presently he starts knocking the
> house about in a way that hurts abominably and does
> not seem to make sense. What on earth is he up to?
> The explanation is that he is building quite a different
> house from the one you thought of—throwing out a
> new wing here, putting on an extra floor there, run-
> ning up towers, making courtyards. You thought you
> were going to be made into a decent little cottage: but
> he is building a palace. He intends to come and live in
> it himself.[2]

CHAPTER THREE

PLAYING CHEETAH

It was a misty, overcast day. Here and there dense black clouds threatened to turn the soft drizzle into torrents of rain. As if in response to the uncertain atmosphere, traffic on one of the most crowded of all California freeways moved more slowly and less predictably than ever. It was, in general, a good day to stay home! Yet with a sense of illogical logic that such was the pathway to tranquility, my friend and I battled the elements and the Los Angeles freeways to meet a third friend for tea. We had planned this escape for a week; in recent days, the pressures of life had been unusually heavy. Now, no inconvenience of weather, distance, or traffic jams was going to stop us from a much-needed break.

As we drove off the freeway and down the coast toward the hotel where we were to meet our friend, even the ocean appeared gray. Yet as we approached the hotel and watched the waves washing up over the beach below, once again, as always, the sea began to have its calming effect on me.

To complete the scene, the hotel lobby, with its great bowls of flowers and its crackling fireplace inside, added a contrast of cheerfulness to the gray skies and the turbulent sea outside, a contrast I have always found to be enormously uplifting. The knot in my stomach relaxed, and I no longer felt in a hurry. The safety zone of afternoon tea with good friends in a relaxing atmosphere was beginning to have its positive effect.

As we waited to be seated, a lady in front of us turned to her friend and said, "This morning I felt in such turmoil I knew that if I didn't plan this I wasn't going to make it." Her friend smiled understandingly and agreed that she, too, had known such days.

The friend we came to meet was late. She was the only one of us who didn't have the day off, and so she was rushing to get away from work as early as possible. After some time went by, a telephone message was relayed to us explaining that she was late but on her way.

Enjoying the luxury of a whole day off, I felt a twinge of guilt. If you rush too much to get to a safety zone, the safety zone can become just another high wire, another demand that adds to rather than detracts from the demands of life. I thought that perhaps I should call my friend and tell her that we understood if she couldn't make it, but I didn't have her work number with me. So we waited.

We finally sat down and waited for our tea to steep while we continued to wait for our friend. I looked out the window at the sea once again, and I felt the tranquility of the scene: the sea outside, the warmth inside, and the serenity of just doing nothing. Steeping tea cannot be hurried. It takes its time, no matter what the immediacy of the situation. Maybe that's part of what makes taking tea have such great potential for providing a safety zone. It slows us down. It forces either contemplation or conversation.

Then I looked across the room and saw my friend approaching. "This is just what I need," she commented, with the conspiratorial smile of one who has escaped in spite of many obstacles. "I'm so glad I didn't give up on coming," she said, and I was glad I hadn't called and discouraged her. The three of us had all needed a safety zone that provided a break from the everyday pressure. We didn't need, nor could we take, a vacation in the south of France, but we did need that minibreak that can make, in a cumulative way, the difference between going on and burning out. If burnout can come in small increments, so can relief be provided by many small occasions of relief.

Burnout is the current buzzword that simply reiterates a condition that has always been a problem for those who have too much to do and too little time in which to do it. The old truism that if you want something done right, find someone who's busy has always been accurate. Out of this truth comes the basis for burnout.

Some of us have tired of the word *burnout*, partly because the word has become so overused that it has come to mean everything from overwork to laziness and boredom. I have had people consult me after two days on a job complaining of burnout. Now, it is possible to feel that you have the wrong job after two days of work, but it is not possible to be truly burned out! Similarly, students who never study but feel burned out at school may have a problem with school but not with burnout.

High-wire living, walking on water, and *doing it all* are more apt descriptions to me of what is commonly called *burnout.* Whatever we call it, however, none of us is equipped to cope with the condition of top-speed living in the fast lane. Even in a society where an ulcer is a badge of executive success and how far you travel and how late you work are sometimes confused with efficiency, none of us can do it all. We must make tough decisions. We must choose priorities.

Sometimes the decisions are agonizing and very personal. About ten years ago I came very close to adopting a child. The further I got in the paper work, the more I slowed down. Then I realized that *for me,* with the absorption I had in my work, I could not add a small child to my life. If I did, my work would suffer or the child would lack nurturing.

A few years ago a man I distantly knew intrigued me. He seemed to be able to do it all at a time when I had become completely convinced that sensible living was the only long-range way to plan one's life. He was raising a large family, had a high-powered career, conducted seminars on his days off, and was very active in a large church. Secretly I envied his endurance and was tempted to think that if I tried a little harder maybe I could walk on water too. Fortunately, I didn't change my life-style because of him. Two years later, he had a heart attack and developed a chronic disease that will slow him down for the rest of his life. He just *looked* as if he could walk on water. He couldn't; none of us can.

Burnout, trying to walk on water as a way of life, doesn't

work for anyone. Students who stay up all night studying for tests usually don't do as well in their classes as students who consistently study and get proper sleep. My writing goes better when I plan it out over a period of months and don't try to do it all at one time. The quality of my work improves, and the stress on my body is incredibly reduced. In the long run we accomplish more, both in quantity and in quality, by steadiness and pacing, and certainly we last longer.

In a striking statement about our inability to do it all, Samuel Rutherford once wrote, "There is but a certain quality of spiritual force in any man. Spread it over a broad surface, the stream is shallow and languid; narrow the channel and it becomes a driving force." In connection with this statement, missionary Amy Carmichael added, "We must learn to plough deep rather than wide. Only God can plough both deep and wide." Indeed, Jesus Christ, God-Man, is the only One who has ever walked on water. Walking on water is not the province of mortal man.

High-wire living not only affects our work adversely, but also can damage our relationships with other people. Friends who commit to accommodating everyone's needs and try to do it all fail at some point out of sheer exhaustion and, in spite of all their efforts, in the end disappoint people because of that failure.

I hear people make statements like "Call me any hour of the night if you need me." I cringe inside, not because I doubt the value of being available for someone who is in a real state of crisis, but because I hear these same people say this to almost everyone they talk to. Then, if too many people take them up on their offer, they back off, usually abruptly and without warning. The end result is that through their overextension they end up hurting the people they most wanted to help, while they themselves feel guilty and a bit resentful over what they now view as "being used."

The marital relationship is probably the most sensitive, intimate human relationship in this world. As such it is also the human relationship most vulnerable to hurt and most able to give joy. Those who try to have it all by making their spouses do more than they can manage can very easily end up destroying their marriages.

Repeatedly in my counseling office I see couples in which the wife wants the husband to get out and make more money, and at the same time she wants him to do more household tasks and spend more time with their children. The man ends up in my office defensive and angry because he's tried to do it all and it wasn't enough.

In a similar way, men who want their wives to work full-time often expect them to continue to maintain all the household tasks and to assume full care of the children. One woman I know just quit her job. Her husband had forced her into a job she hadn't even wanted and then refused to give up his three nights of volleyball each week in order to baby-sit while she worked. He still can't figure out why she "won't do her share."

People who try to walk on water generally drown; while they sink, many others stand by and criticize or wonder what's wrong with the person. Only a few are perceptive enough to see that this person isn't weak but just doing too much. By the time he or she reaches my counseling office, the would-be water-walker has thoroughly bought into the idea of being "weak" and is making statements like "If I were stronger, I could have done this" or, depending on his orientation, "If I were a better Christian, I wouldn't be here." They feel as though they did all they could do and more, and it wasn't enough. Their self-images are down, their bodies are sick, and they don't feel up to trying harder. To declare their boundaries is not in their vocabulary, and so they feel like hopeless failures.

It becomes the obligation of counseling to help people set realistic boundaries while they learn to declare those boundaries to others. In her speech at the Wellesley commencement ceremonies in 1990, First Lady Barbara Bush exhorted the graduates to choose their priorities in life carefully. If we can't do it all, we can at least make wise choices. Mrs. Bush warned, "At the end of your life, you will never regret not having passed one more test, not winning one more verdict, or not closing one more deal. You will regret time not spent with a husband, a child, a friend or a parent. . . ."

Sometimes our families want fewer things from us: smaller houses, cheaper clothes, and more modest forms of entertainment. Sometimes those we love most just want more of us and our time rather than the material extras we can give them by working two jobs. A young child who had been rescued from a series of abusive situations was at last living safely with his father. Their house was located in a modest neighborhood. They lived in financially tight circumstances, but each member of the family was surrounded by much love. Coming home late one night, as the car turned the corner on their street, the child murmured sleepily, "Daddy, I just love this street." He hadn't noticed that the houses were old and needed painting or that the sidewalks were cracked. He didn't seem to mind sharing his room with two brothers. He just knew that on this street he was loved, and love made the street beautiful to him.

To a limited extent, high-wire living has some legitimate function, and it is not always neurotically motivated. A crisis or an emergency can warrant the use of a high-wire response. The response is not meant to be long-range, however. A forest fire, for example, requires everyone who is nearby to do anything possible *until* added help arrives. On the domestic front, a woman who is a single parent and who goes to an office at nine every morning may find that she needs to spend an occasional sleepless night with a sick child. If the illness extends itself over a period of time, she cannot continue the nightly vigil as well as her job. At this point she will need to get off the high wire by finding someone to help with the child or by taking a few days off work.

Accidents, illnesses, earthquakes, and floods—as well as smaller occurrences, like stopped-up drains, family arguments, complaints from neighbors, and calls from a child's teacher—comprise the types of extraordinary events that require a response that is not planned into our ordinary daily schedule. However, if we are living well-planned lives with time out for rest and recreation, these emergencies, both small and large, will not overwhelm us as much. We will have a reserve we can use to meet them. If we are already overwhelmed and living close to the edge of our emotional and physical resources on a daily basis, however, these added pressures will seem insurmountable. Even a broken faucet will become too much to cope with.

Normal life itself, without any emergencies, has a limited high-wire quality scattered throughout. Any job worth doing intensifies our efforts at certain points. When I write, for example, I rarely stay passive. My intensity builds to the point where my topic consumes me. The subject matter is, at that moment, the most important thing in the world to me. Without that, my writing becomes passive and flat.

Passion makes all of us better at what we are doing, whether we are planning a school play, baking bread, drawing up plans for a new house, performing surgery, or selling cars. Depending on the amount of intensity involved, however, times of rest and recreation must punctuate the activity. How effectively we alternate these rest periods with the work periods will determine whether burnout occurs. Jobs ordinarily have break periods and paid vacations for this reason.

The danger starts when we begin to work through lunch, skip breaks, landscape our yards, or take classes during our vacation times. Sometimes exceptions can be made. For someone who works at an accounting firm most of the year, painting the house during a vacation can be a useful change, as long as it does not become a pattern for every vacation. Working late to meet a deadline is legitimate, as long as the additional hours are the exception rather than the rule.

The life-style of the cheetah is very instructive to those of us who tend to try to do it all. In the opinion of most experts, the cheetah is the fastest animal on earth. At its peak it can run up to seventy miles an hour. It is a magnificent sight to watch the cheetah run at top speed, flexing its powerful muscles as it seems to glide over the land and barely touch the ground. Its speed enables the cheetah to be a remarkable hunter. Yet it can maintain that speed for only a short time. Then it stops totally in order to regain the strength to run seventy miles an hour once again.

Like the cheetah, if we run seventy miles an hour, we must stop every now and then. The trouble with many of us is that we think we can continue running at seventy miles an hour without ever stopping. Then, when we fall, we feel as though we are weak, as though we have failed. The problem was that we played cheetah by rushing at top speed, but we didn't play cheetah when it was time to stop for a while. If you are going to run like a cheetah, you have to stop like a cheetah.

My dog, Horace, is a small sheltie with a big-dog personality. Keeping vigil over the apartment where I live is his full-time task. He expends a prodigious amount of energy racing from window to window, watching those who come and go, and barking fiercely at intruders. Horace's intense life-style competes with the cheetah's seventy-miles-per-hour life-style. He provides a constant example to me of high-wire intensity personified.

Yet, like the cheetah, Horace can shut down from high speed to complete immobility in a matter of seconds. When he sleeps, his repose is so deep that you have to touch him or shout to wake him up. Horace runs like a cheetah, but he also stops like a cheetah. In this way he constantly renews his energy.

Some of us work quickly by nature. We love our work and we tend to want to keep going at it. We, more than anyone else, need to learn to play cheetah. Winston Churchill once wrote quite succinctly of those who have heavy responsibilities and of their need for relief: "Change is the master key."[1]

Consistent with that thought, people who work inside may need to go outside for recreation. Teachers may not want to teach Sunday school. Housepainters will not find rest by painting their own houses on weekends. They may have to do it now and then, but it will be work for them, not recreation.

One person's relaxation may be another person's work. In marriage counseling I find that a big problem between spouses is their lack of perception of the other's needs at the end of a day. On the one hand, the person who comes home from an office building often wants quiet and rest. Providing a forty-five-minute period of isolation from any demands, including those of the children, or becoming a listener for that person will usually solve the problem.

On the other hand, the person who has been at home all day, cleaning, cooking, and talking to three-year-old minds, needs companionship and even excitement. Watching a movie after the children are in bed, a late-night talk over cups of hot chocolate, or occasionally hiring a baby-sitter for an evening out will generally help to alleviate the tensions of the day for that person. However, rather than giving each other what they need by a process of give-and-take, the tendency is to argue instead. Then both partners feel misunderstood and alone.

Once they see that the other person's needs are different from their own, much progress can be made in counseling couples who have this type of problem. Furthermore, if learning to express such needs and becoming perceptive to a spouse's changing needs are the result of spending time in the safety zone of counseling, then, as children grow older and perhaps both spouses go out to work, the couple will be able to perceive on their own the resulting changes in their needs and think of ways to meet their new needs.

Therefore, playing cheetah is not only planning our lives realistically and resting physically. Playing cheetah is also finding activities that provide change from our normal routine. It is important to know ourselves. A forest ranger might find relaxation in city life; someone living in the middle of Manhattan might need a lake or a mountain range.

Churchill also provides valuable insight on the different needs of those who like their work and those who just do their jobs routinely. Those who enjoy what they are doing are, according to Churchill, "Fortune's favoured children. . . . For them the working hours are never long enough. Each day is a holiday, and ordinary holidays when they come are grudged as enforced interruptions in an absorbing vocation." Although both groups need to play cheetah, and both need change and relaxation, "It may well be that those whose work is their pleasure are those who most need the means of banishing it at intervals from their minds."[2] It is difficult to break away from an absorbing task.

Coming from a different time than Churchill, and certainly more entrenched in the Puritan work ethic, the famous preacher Charles Spurgeon wrote with amazing balance on the subject of refurbishment after labor. In comparing such needs with the animal world, he cautioned that even animals eat and lie down after their activity. Where Churchill stresses change, Spurgeon stresses quietness and meditation upon God, but both saw the need for balancing work with rest. Both saw the need for diversion.

In contrast to the feelings of failure that arise from burnout, Spurgeon promises, "You will return to your business in a better spirit; you may expect (other things being equal) to earn more that day, than you ever earned before, by the painful system of uninterrupted drudgery; for the diversion of thought will rest, string up, and brace your nerves, and enable you to do more work, and do it better too." [3]

Many delusions are connected with trying to do it all. When I was a college student, I took a full load at the university and a partial load at a Bible seminary—at the same time! I also taught Sunday school, dated several times a week, and held part-time jobs on campus. To top it off, I graduated early. I did all this with the help of several delusions, the major one being that if it looked okay on paper it would work. I arranged my classes at the university for Monday, Wednesday, and Friday. I went to the seminary on Tuesday and Thursday. Work fit in between classes during what I called "extra" time. Church and dating were necessary recreation, I reasoned. However, the plan didn't work. I made it through school, but I ran down my physical resources in the process. I was, in the best definition of the term, *burned out*. At the root of my problems was the attitude that if it looked good written on a schedule it would work.

One problem with my schedule was that it didn't allow enough time for rest. It counted activities like teaching children as recreation, when in actuality they were work. It didn't allow for traffic jams, bouts of flu, telephone calls, cooking, extra academic assignments, favors for friends, or even just time to *be*.

For me, at least, this trying to walk on water also got

confused with what looked like the will of God. After all, what better way could an eighteen-year-old use her time than by going to Bible seminary and teaching Sunday school? I hadn't learned what many people I counsel never learn: to choose between the good and the good. It is easy to clear our lives of so-called bad things; it's much harder to say no to the good.

Entering into this way of thinking is what psychologist Rollo May has called the Messiah Complex. Good people often feel that a need constitutes an obligation. If there is a legitimate need, they must meet it. Underneath this mentality is the idea that if I don't do it, nobody else will. Good people need to confront the needs around them by asking, "Is this a need I am meant to meet?" We need more of that helping attitude in this world. Indeed, such an attitude is a basic Christian characteristic. However, beware of assuming that if there is a need you must meet it. As Christians we must be led more specifically than that.

The late J. B. Phillips, a noted Bible translator, was a good example of a man tortured by what appears to be, at least in part, burnout. As I read of his life, a flashing red light came on when I learned that for a long time Dr. Phillips took on every request for speaking as a leading from God. The need constituted a call from God. The result was burnout from which he never really recovered.

Motives for water-walking are numerous. For some of us, high-wire living has an appeal that simply fits our personalities and perhaps goes back as far as our childhood years. There is so much to do and so little time to do it. One day when I was looking through the slips of paper and clippings my mother had kept in her well-worn Bible,

I found one on which my mother had written, "Elizabeth said today (at age four), 'I'm too busy to sleep.' " Reading that brief note reinforced my conviction that slowing down has always been a struggle for me. At the same time, learning to pace my life has been one of my greatest personal victories.

Sometimes, too, as in the example of Dr. Phillips, the needs that a certain person can uniquely fill seem so pressing. I'm sure that in times of national crisis or catastrophic disaster, people with outstanding, rare talents face a constant threat of burnout.

Trying to walk on water is a problem that builds upon so many seemingly unrelated issues. When it is based on obvious factors, like temperament or unique, crisis-type needs that press in from outside, even then, no matter how much we enjoy what we are doing, and no matter how genuine and even worthwhile the demands of the crisis, eventually we must play cheetah and stop. Walking on water cannot become a life-style if we are going to survive.

On a more neurotic level, certain people just can't say no, even when they want to. For others, an overly busy schedule seems to indicate success or being needed. For them, burnout becomes a status symbol. For these people, high-wire living relates, at least partially, to low self-esteem and problems with declaring, since secure people are more likely to be realistic about their capacities and able to declare their boundaries once they know how.

Burnout relates also to one's spiritual beliefs in the sense that many people who burn out have the false belief that they are burning out for God. Paradoxically, rather than viewing God as a motivating force in burnout, we often need divine guidance to discern when to say no. Then it may take special divine strength to utter the word *No*.

Neurotic guilt is a very real issue in burnout, and many people who seek counseling relate experiences of over-committing simply because they did not want to deal with guilt feelings. Guilt is often confused with spiritual issues because of a failure to differentiate between neurotic and realistic guilt. When I feel guilty because I have done something wrong, I need forgiveness. Then I need to change my behavior so that I do not make the same mistake again. In contrast, neurotic guilt is not based on actual wrong-doing but on what is imagined. For those who experience a sense of neurotic guilt, saying no can be a painful experience because it starts the tapes playing: *If I were a stronger person I could do this,* or *How can I say no when there is no one else to meet the need?* or just *What if my friends don't like me because I've said no?*

For many, trying to do it all is simply a way of avoiding the space and quietness of stopping. For them, burnout is the classic symptom of the disease of our time, loneliness. Loneliness, in turn, connects with other factors that affect burnout, such as self-esteem and spiritual wholeness. The best antidotes for loneliness are to like ourselves enough to enjoy being alone and to have a personal relationship with God.

From the point of view of a counselor, the sad part about water-walkers is that they always do too much and feel strung out and tired, yet they never feel they do enough. To do so much and then to fail is the fate of water walking. To play cheetah is, in simple language, the cure.

Then comes the most Christian challenge of all: to do good just for the sake of doing good. It is easy to feed the poor whenever a neurotic need to save the world drives us to it; it's harder when we do it only because it's the right thing to do. It's easy to sit up half the night on the phone with a distressed person when having that person call us with a problem makes us feel needed. But when we already feel needed, and someone reaches out to us to talk at an inconvenient time, it takes the love of God to extend ourselves.

Therefore, although a low self-image drives a great many people to contradictory and often destructive behavior, having good mental health is an awesome responsibility. For good mental health expands the opportunity for choice, whereas bad mental health limits personal choice. I see children, for example, who react in very diverse ways when they feel neglected by their parents. One child may go on a high wire, overachieve in school, and compete to almost impossible extremes in sports just to please his parents. When the parents don't even notice his achievements, the child may become bitter or hopeless, or he may decide that he'll build a life for himself in spite of his parents' neglect.

Another child in the same family may react to the neglect with clear-cut anger: acts of violence, neighborhood vandalism, or membership in a gang where he *does* feel important. Still a third child in the same family may become withdrawn and daydream a lot, or he may become depressed and even suicidal.

How a given child responds to neglect depends on that child's position in the family, how the child perceives the neglect, and personal temperament, as well as outside factors such as a concerned schoolteacher or a talent for art combined with the opportunity to develop that talent.

All the behaviors produced in such a family, however, have one root cause: feelings of low self-worth resulting from parental neglect. Trying to walk on water in order to compensate is only one of the possible symptoms.

In contrast, good mental health tends to take away the neurotic need to prove ourselves, to take revenge for past wrongs, or to feel constantly guilty even when any realistic reason for guilt is removed. Good mental health enables free choice, and with free choice comes the obligation to do right.

Choosing to do good rather than being driven to it means the difference between a life lived in chaos and a life lived with order and control. Furthermore, morality that arises from choice rather than bondage receives greater reward from God. After all, there's not much virtue involved in doing something just because you can't say no.

A colleague once told me of a patient he had been seeing who had lived for years on high wires. His health run down, he had finally sought professional help. After several months of therapy, one morning the man suddenly commented on the beauty of a red geranium that was blooming outside the doctor's office. "It's always been there," my friend replied. "You've just never noticed it." Seeing the red geranium was the first indication the patient gave of real progress toward normal living. For the first time in years, the man had literally stopped long enough to smell the flowers.

Even if we are not actually living on a high wire, sometimes we don't realize how fast we have been going. My encounter with the ocean following my recent surgery once again helped me put my life into perspective. I was physically weak and in some pain. Worst of all for me, my thinking was foggy from the anesthesia and pain medication. I had planned to use this time of recuperation for thinking about book ideas and organizing my current writing schedule. If I couldn't see my patients, I had naively assumed with the ignorance of one who has never before had major surgery, I could at least have more time to write and think about writing. It didn't work that way, and for the first time in a long while I had to be content with doing nothing.

Three days after surgery I slowly put a day's effort into walking outside and up some stairs at my motel to a table surrounded by lawn chairs. Exhausted by the exertion, I relaxed into one of the chairs and looked out at the ocean in front of me. This time the sea was bright blue and the sky was sunny. A couple of sailboats drifted by slowly. The moderately high waves, tipped with foam, came in toward me and then disappeared from my view under the grassy cliffs. The cycle repeated itself with a kind of hypnotic monotony. Farther out, the sea looked blue and calm, stretching back into a sky that seemed to come down to meet it. Overhead, the sea gulls flew back and forth, like choreographed beings used as stage props to enhance the beauty of the sea with its painted ships and to add their sounds in a kind of symphony with the waves.

As I watched the scene, I realized how long it had been since I had really *seen* the sea. I thought I had watched it. Certainly it had uplifted me often. However, not for years had I just sat quietly and absorbed its beauty—not looking for inspiration, not looking for anything really. As I slowly made my way back down the steps toward my room, I realized that the sight of that blue ocean, always there, always the same, had quieted my restlessness.

I tried to use the time of my illness for a time of productivity, and I found that instead I had been forced to play cheetah and stop altogether. Yet, strangely enough, the time had not been wasted at all. I had seen the majesty of the sea and had reflected on the One under whose control we all remain. When once again I returned to my work, it was with a sense of renewal that I had not known in a long time.

CHAPTER FOUR

A SAFETY ZONE OF DISCOVERY

"What rock do I lean on all week when you aren't there?" The question, thrown out as a parting statement, left me a little stunned with its directness. Sara had just finished her first counseling session with me. She impressed me as being a very intelligent lady, even though she wouldn't have agreed. In truth, Sara had a very low opinion of herself, an opinion reflected in her lack of care in dressing and in the flow of demeaning remarks she made about herself. "People don't like me, and I don't blame them" was a good example of her low self-esteem.

I was the third in a series of counselors to whom she had turned in her struggle with depression. In her sessions with the first counselor, she had found great comfort in her otherwise isolated existence, but no concrete long-range help. The second counselor had offered greater direction, but Sara had resisted the scariness of growth and change. With me she had found once again that sense of safety and encouragement that should be part of the counseling experience, but she was also once again confronted with the challenge to change. Paradoxically, until that change occurred, Sara would feel vulnerable. As a person who had few other safety zones in her life, when she left a counseling session she might feel that she was leaving her major safety zone. She might again want to ask, "What rock do I lean on when you aren't there?"

Anyone who seeks counseling is at that time in need of a safety zone. Safety zones are anchors. Safety zones help prevent burnout. They include special places, significant people, things, and even ideas that stabilize us in times of uncertainty, comfort us in times of difficulty, and equip us to go on. As a safety zone, counseling should be a place of comfort, protection, and encouragement, but it should be also a place of growth and change, and it must always be a place where people can develop tools that enable them to face life more effectively. It is a place where one can deal with old tapes. It is a place where one can learn to cut tapes or to declare. It is a place of refurbishing.

The safety zone of counseling is normally meant to be temporary; if it becomes a place of permanent residency, the positive benefits turn into stunted growth and destruction. What is a legitimate crutch enabling healing becomes crippling in itself if it is used beyond its time of need. Then what once enabled growth and independence fosters a crippling dependence.

When I was in high school biology, we were asked to do a science project for extra credit. I chose to do one that involved hatching chicken eggs in an incubator. The school lent me an incubator, and I bought fertilized eggs from a nearby hatchery.

At the outset, all went well. For the first few hours and then days, I opened an egg, observed the developing chick under a microscope, and made drawings of what I saw. Then, as the embryos began to grow bigger, I just waited for the day when they would hatch.

By the time Easter vacation arrived, the chicks were overdue. My biology teacher suggested that I take the incubator home for the week. Day after day I waited. Nothing. After three or four days of vacation, I called a hatchery. Their conclusion was that the chicks had died in the shell. The only way to find out was to open one.

Armed with the moral support of a friend, I cautiously picked at one of the shells. No movement. I picked more. Still no movement. Then I saw that the shell contained a full-grown chick, but the chick was dead. Not wanting to take a chance on even one live chick being destroyed, I painstakingly opened each egg. Each one contained a small, dead chick, until I got to the last egg, which, for some reason I don't remember, happened to be that of a duck. Inside there was a slight movement. I was there just in time to get it out before it too died. With a lot of care, the duck survived and became a pet.

When I finished opening the eggs, I was pretty shaken up. So I called the hatchery back to ask why the chicks had died, and I was told that they had died because of lack of moisture. The school incubator had not regulated this factor properly.

For a number of days the eggs had sheltered and nourished these chicks. The embryos had developed the circulatory systems that I had observed under the microscope.

They had been fed by the nutrients in the egg yolk. They had developed little feet and beaks. They had grown to their full size. Then their little place of growth and safety became a death trap. They had stayed there too long.

Nature is full of such illustrations. A young plant that grows and is nurtured in a pot gradually becomes root bound and dies if it stays in that same small pot. The magnificent butterfly develops from the lowly caterpillar only as it breaks out of the chrysalis that has provided shelter but now would cause its death if it remained. The beautiful shell of the chambered nautilus is formed because the small sea creature grows a new chamber each time it outgrows the old. In each case the organism must leave the place that once provided comfort and life itself if it is to survive and grow.

In the same way the safety zone of counseling—as well as other safety zones, like friendship, a favorite restaurant, a weekend retreat, or a relationship with God—is meant to be a place of refurbishment and renewal, a place to go out from and, at times, to return to. Even in our relationship with God, which is our only permanent safety zone, we still don't live in the building where we worship; we don't stay forever on our knees in prayer. We go out from that safety zone into the world, equipped and blessed from our encounter with God. A safety zone is not a comfort zone. It is not a place of self-pity or self-indulgence. It is a place of positive recovery and growth.

Christine, a child of eight, came with her father for his counseling sessions and read books in my waiting room. One day I invited her in alone for a few minutes. She cried while she told me how unhappy she was because her parents argued all the time. She was sure that they were headed for a divorce. After that I managed to get a few minutes alone with her each week, time stolen from her father's time and my break. She usually cried, and I tried to encourage her. I learned from her father that she eagerly anticipated each session, and so I was always careful to spend a little time with her. My office and my relationship became an important safety zone in her life, even with the limitations of time.

One evening after a couple of months had passed, Christine bounced into my office with a huge smile on her face. She flung her coat on a chair, spread out her arms dramatically, and exclaimed, "Boy, this counseling sure works!" I didn't need to ask why. In this instance only one thing would have made her this happy. Her parents weren't fighting anymore. Interestingly enough, the next week Christine chose to stay home and play with a friend rather than see me. For the time, and perhaps forever, Christine had outgrown counseling as her place of comfort and growth. She was going on.

To view counseling as a place incorporates some of the best philosophy that has been developed regarding the basic function of counseling. Psychiatrist Paul Tournier has so beautifully stated:

> The giving of a place to those who have none seems to me to be one way of defining our vocation as healers of persons . . . in helping our patients to find their places we are helping them to become persons. And that place is no abstraction. It is our consulting room, the fireside, the photographs on the mantelpiece, the clock they detest, the books on the shelves, all the little details with which they have become familiar

during those hours that have been so important in
their lives . . . how many patients find it hard to leave
when the consultation is over, to leave this place![1]

If finding a place or, as I like to call it, a safety zone,
provides a basis for emotional healing, then the kind of
uprooting that we find in our life-styles as we approach
the twenty-first century is a cause for our feeling of lack of
place. We buy services, move frequently, change jobs, dis-
pose of friends, and then wonder why we have so few
resources with which to face the ordinary demands of life,
to say nothing of the extraordinary demands involved in
just living in this age of high-tech medicine and nuclear
threat.

For example, what other generation has had to decide
when to turn off a respirator or whether to redefine death?
Fifty years ago all a physician had to do was try to save
lives; when people died, they simply stopped moving. Yet
at the same time what other generation has fought so hard
for independence and then spent so many hours in counseling offices trying to get rid of the resultant feelings of
isolation and loneliness? We long for closeness, but we
fear its price tag.

In further describing this place, this safety zone called
counseling, in what has been for me the best definition of
counseling that I have ever heard, psychologist Rollo May
remains unique in aptness of description. To him the age-
old image of the hearth best conveys the intimacy and
warmth of the counseling relationship:

It is like inviting the traveler from his snowy and
chilly journey to warm himself for an hour before the

fire on another's hearth. Such understanding, it is not too much to say, is the most objective form of love. That is why there is always a tendency on the part of the counselee to feel some love toward the counselor, this person "who understands me." There are few gifts that one person can give another in this world as rich as understanding.[2]

Dr. Tournier uses the same fireside image, but in a more literal way:

When people come to see me in order to know and understand themselves better I interview them at my fireside. . . . For all of us the fire in the hearth is a powerful symbol, full of poetic meaning: it gives warmth, it is alive, it dies down and burns up again, it must be stirred, it is fascinating; it is a focus, a radiant center.[3]

The intimacy of the hearth brings the definition of *counseling* close to that of *friendship*, even though it goes without saying that it must also be an ideal and safe friendship with more than the usual structure, boundaries, and goals. Still, at its basis a good counseling relationship includes many of the same qualities as a good friendship. Sometimes counseling is merely a substitute for what could be accomplished in a close friendship.

In times of extreme stress human beings have survived only in strong supportive groups, in the safety zone of relationships. In our recent history, the Holocaust still offers some of the most striking examples of this. A recent study of survivors of Hitler's concentration camps states:

Friendship was essential to survival, especially
within the little groups which were constituted—
groups of three or four people—our "families," as we
called them. There were a few people who remained
isolated, and they died. You simply couldn't survive
alone.[4]

In a remarkable little book, *Dachau Sermons*, Lutheran
pastor and concentration camp survivor Martin Niemöller
described the meeting together of several inmates in the
concentration camp where he himself was imprisoned.
During several years of confinement in one of Hitler's
camps, the meetings in Cell 34 amounted to only "six
vacation hours!" Those who met were a Dutch cabinet
minister, two Norwegian shippers, a British major, a Yu-
goslavian diplomat, and a Macedonian journalist. They
were Calvinists, Lutherans, Anglicans, and Greek Ortho-
dox. In a Communion service held on Maundy Thursday,
March 29, 1945, Pastor Niemöller said to those who had
gathered in Cell 34 in Dachau concentration camp:

To this great community of those who proclaim the
death of their Lord as a message of joy belong this
evening also we, who come here to his table. A small
company, every one of us torn away from his earthly
home and from the circle of his dear ones, all of us
robbed of freedom and ever uncertain about what the
following day or even the following hour will bring.
But, despite all this, we are at home. We eat and
drink at the table of our heavenly Father and we may
be comforted. There is nothing that could tear us
away and separate us from him, since our Lord and
Master gave his life for us and for many, indeed, even

for both of the friends who have gone away from our circle and whom we remember in our intercession, even for our dear ones far away or out there at the fronts, for whom we are anxious. For them also did the Lord die, and with him they and we are well protected.[5]

In the fellowship of God and in the company of a few of His believers, this man who had been imprisoned in his own country for standing against that country's evil could say, "We are at home."

At the same time in history, friendships that were of an intensity and intimacy of trust common to a good counseling relationship also provided a safety zone to those outside of the camps who were part of the resistance movement. A Dutch woman, Miep Gies, was largely responsible for hiding Anne Frank and her family in Holland. As the war continued, just getting food for those she was hiding as well as for her husband, Henk, and herself was a major task. They did without and there was little time to focus on anything but survival for themselves, the Frank family, and the others in hiding with them.

Miep and Henk became friends with a Dutch couple who lived across the street from them. Sometimes the four of them would sit up late to drink a coffee substitute and listen, illegally, to the BBC.

One night Miep and Henk were feeling particularly discouraged. On impulse, Miep took the last of the real coffee she had hidden away, grabbed Henk's hand, and, after curfew, dashed across the street to share it with their friends. Showing the result of not just coffee but of the

safety zone of closeness and trust that existed in contrast
to the hell around them, Miep recalled:

> Making each drop of rich coffee last as long as pos-
> sible, we savored, in every way, the smell, taste, ef-
> fect. It worked like magic. Soon, we were animated
> and again full of spit and vinegar against the German
> oppressor. Once again we were no longer beaten
> down, just biding our time until the Allies could get
> to us. . . . We had made good use of our last real
> coffee.[6]

The safety zone of relationships had comforted them
and then sent them out into the dark night of Hitler's war,
refurbished and able to go on.

Even in so-called normal life, none of us lives unto ourselves. We still need the safety zone of relationships that
feed us and nurture us. English pubs are an example of
people getting together casually after a day's work, cele-
brating the small triumphs of each day, and commiserat-
ing together over the failures. It is said that once a week,
on Tuesday, C. S. Lewis, J. R. R. Tolkien, and Charles
Williams met together at their favorite Oxford pub, the
Eagle and Child. There they talked about their writing,
speculated on ideas, and drank beer. Sometimes, too, the
Inklings, as this group called itself, met in Lewis's rooms
at Magdalen College at Oxford.

In referring to one such meeting of the Inklings, Lewis
wrote of his conversion, "I have just passed on from believing in God to definitely believing in Christ—in Christianity. I will try to explain this another time. My long
night talk with Dyson and Tolkien had a good deal to do
with it."[7] Such is the potential of a safety zone.

In America many seek a bar after work because they cannot bear to leave the pressure of the workplace only to trade it for the pressure of the home—or the loneliness of the home in some cases. One suspects, however, that the focus is less on beer and more on hard liquor and that the ideas discussed do not normally attempt the height of those of the Oxford Inklings.

In the classic movie *Harvey*, James Stewart describes how his imaginary rabbit, Harvey, and he go into a bar and sit down, and pretty soon people turn to him and smile:

> We've entered as strangers. Soon we have friends . . . they tell about the big, terrible things they've done and the big, wonderful things they'll do. Their hopes, their regrets, their loves and their hates . . . all very large because nobody ever brings anything small into a bar.

Clubs and coffee shops provide places where people gather, not so much for the food but for the community with other people. Afternoon tea, too, provides a break in the monotony or the pressure of the everyday work schedule. These become places of reprieve, and as such they are often fiercely defended. Perhaps this is why men who normally see women as their equals defend the right to have exclusively male clubs. It is not an issue of equality to them; it is a matter of defending the sacredness and sameness of this place that refurbishes them.

After the death of my Aunt Esther, I and my Uncle Blanton, with whom I had always been close, met together every Monday night at a coffee shop. Sometimes

we ate dinner, but more often we just had pie and coffee. For him, in particular, it was a weekly safety zone in
which to express grief; for both of us it was a time to talk
over the week and to debate ideas. "Jonesie," as I called
him, had never gone to college, but he had knowledge
equal to at least one Ph.D., and we could go on for
hours discussing writing ideas and Christian theology.
The time was a safety zone for both of us, one that I miss
to this day. It was a safety zone of normal life, for it was
not crisis oriented.

The support of others and the good counsel of caring
friends are what most of us need most of the time. Indeed,
for most of us the question is not whether we will ever be
involved in a counseling situation but rather how formal
that counseling will be. There are times, however, when
training and skill are required. Then we need the safety
zone of more formalized counseling, which still comforts
but also deals with the specific problem at hand, like a
bout of depression or a troublesome relationship, and goes
on to equip us to so deal with the world around us that
future problems are minimized.

The situations that demand professional counseling are
as varied as the individuals involved. Steven was a successful businessman. At his work as a salesman, the demands to perform were heavy. At home his wife's desire
for possessions and social status was equally heavy. Both
his wife and his boss had quick tempers and sharp
tongues. Arguments got Steve nowhere because nasty
words and shouting, rather than reason, were the weap-
ons of the day.

After ten days of hospitalization with chest pains,
Steven consulted me. Some techniques on how to deal

with demanding people were the main focus of the counseling, along with help in building up Steven's low self-image, which had enabled those around him to intimidate him. Steven needed to learn to declare. The support of friends alone could not have solved Steven's problems.

Lucinda was only five years old, but her mother brought her to see me after she had been diagnosed as having an ulcer. Lucy's parents were divorced, but otherwise she didn't seem to have any unusual negative factors in her environment. Certainly there was nothing that seemed to warrant an ulcer at age five!

During her second appointment, Lucy and I played with a large dollhouse I have in my office. For some children the dollhouse is simply a source of pleasure that relaxes them enough to talk. For others the play is revealing. Lucy focused on the father doll. She moved him upstairs to live. She had the other members of the doll family try to make him feel better. Then, in her play, one night he disappeared, and she explained to me that the doll-father had been murdered.

Translated into real life, it turned out that Lucy's father had indeed disappeared, and Lucy had decided that he had been murdered. When I asked her directly if she felt that her father had been murdered, she replied with a quick yes. Her father did write an occasional letter to his sister, but no one had bothered to tell Lucy, nor had she asked. Once I told her about these letters and she knew that her father was alive, the ulcer vanished. All she needed after that was the love and understanding that her family could best give to her.

Stephanie was a middle-aged woman with crippling fears of almost everything, from standing in line at the bank to sleeping alone at night. Once again her problems and her treatment were unique. For Stephanie the key was in an undiagnosed metabolic imbalance, the diagnosis and treatment of which speeded up the counseling process. Today Stephanie is successful as a teacher, and she can barely relate to her former fears.

Some people feel that counseling must focus on the past in order to be effective. To the contrary, although the past often gives insight into the present, becoming tangled up in the tapes of the past can actually exacerbate a problem rather than relieve it. To know that you fear elevators because you were stuck in one at age three may be interesting for the insight it provides, but from what I have observed, it rarely rids you of the fear.

There are, at times, exceptions. The girl who consulted me regarding her seemingly unfounded hatred for her mother told me a little about her childhood. When she described her father's death from a heart attack, which occurred when she was only ten, she told how she saw her mother give her father some medication within seconds of his death. "She killed him," she exclaimed suddenly, "and I miss my father so much!"

After she had calmed down a little, I pointed out to her that maybe her mother had been trying to save her father's life, not take it. "I never thought of that," she admitted. "My mother and father fought a lot, and I was usually on my father's side. So I thought she killed him." One session with the mother clarified the situation to the girl. Her mother had given her husband a nitroglycerin pill, hoping to stop the attack. The mother and daughter still had problems to work out, but now that was possible. In this case, the basis for the solution was to be found in the past.

When events in the past are troublesome, at times understanding them better in the light of today may be helpful. Yet, more often than not, dwelling on the past just
replays, once again, events that were harmful then and
are still harmful now. Remembering how you were molested by your uncle, or how your mother didn't believe
you when you told her, or how much you resented the
favoritism shown to your older brother doesn't usually do
much except make you feel as if it were happening all over
again. Once again, it's one thing to know that you are
afraid of elevators because you were trapped in one at age
three. It's quite another thing to cure the fear. The insight
is merely interesting. It is not a cure.

In recent years a number of concentration camp survivors have committed suicide. "Why now?" one might ask,
a question for which there might be many answers. Yet
many of these individuals who killed themselves were his-
torians or writers. One can only wonder if, with the re-
vival of interest in World War II and the subsequent
references to the atrocities of the camps, for at least these
very vocal individuals, the old tapes of the past didn't get
out of control. "Letting it all hang out" may have stirred
up emotions which have caused old wounds to open up
and fester.

Even though he is viewed as the father of psychoanalysis, Freud himself was the first to acknowledge the limitations of a therapy that analyzed the past. He spoke of
the day when dealing with a person's body chemistry
would be a pivotal factor in the treatment of emotional
disturbances. Then he said, "But for the moment we have
nothing better at our disposal than the technique of psychoanalysis, and for that reason, in spite of its limitations,

it is not to be despised."[8] Today many of us believe that, apart from or in conjunction with physical treatment of the body, there are quicker and more effective techniques than psychoanalysis that can be used to treat psychological problems.

In addition to believing that psychological help must be done through analyzing the past, many feel that counseling must be painful in order to work. In contrast, many of the people I see who feel better after their counseling sessions and look forward to them are often the ones who receive the greatest benefit. You don't have to get worse to feel better. I always feel good when someone leaves my office and says, "I feel so much better than I did when I came in." For some it is the first time that they've ever really noticed a flower in bloom as they walked to their car, or stopped to look up at a cloud formation in the sky. One of the positive fringe benefits of good mental health is freedom to look out from inside oneself to the world around, to see nature, and to feel a oneness with other human beings.

When I was a teenager, I had a remarkable English teacher who possessed this kind of appreciation of life. She used to write quotations on the blackboard, and often I copied them into a notepad that I still have. One such quotation expressed the simple joy of ordinary human life and challenged the reader to grasp that ordinariness while it still exists:

> Normal day, let me be aware of the treasure you are. Let me learn from you, savor you, bless you before you depart. Let me not pass you by in quest of some rare and perfect tomorrow. Let me hold you

while I may, for it will not always be so. One day I shall dig my nails into the earth, or bury my face in the pillow, or stretch myself taut, or raise my hands to the sky, and want more than all the world your return.

Mary Jane Irion

The growth that occurs in the safety zone of counseling enables human beings to live closer to their highest potential. Moreover, it also frees them from themselves enough to enjoy simple pleasures. It should liberate them from bondage to the tapes of "What if?" and "Why not?" It should enable them to be free enough of their own self-concerns to care what happens to another human being and to worship God because of who He is, rather than what He can give.

Such growth does not proceed in a straight line. There is no exact formula for change, for each individual person is unique. Change is new, and new is scary. However, it is wonderful to go out from the hearth, this place of safety, feeling better equipped to deal with life. It is wonderful to realize that what we don't like about ourselves we can change and to see, for perhaps the first time, that we have qualities we can truly respect.

Those of us who are Christians believe in the importance of each individual human being. In an eloquent expression of that importance, the singer and actress Ethel Waters said, "My father raped my mother when she was twelve and, you know what, they're dedicating a park to me in Lancaster, Pennsylvania."[9]

A young girl came into my office after her parents had thrown her out. Catharine was bright, capable, and pretty, but all she could say was, "There must be something wrong with me. Even my parents don't want me." Catharine was a young adult by the time I met her, but childhood abuse and neglect had made her feel that she had no worth at all.

Session after session went by. Catharine enjoyed the counseling sessions, but she didn't change. She was sure that even I, if I really knew her, would agree that she was no good.

One afternoon, as she was telling me about her belief in God, I suddenly threw out a question to her: "Do you believe God makes junk?"

"Of course not," she replied indignantly. "God wouldn't do that."

"But He made you," I countered.

There was a long silence. Then a slight grin. The resistance had been broken through. Catharine had started to make her way back from a lifetime of self-hate. The turning point had been her belief in a God who didn't make junk. The setting for that discovery had been a counseling session that, for her, had become a safety zone of discovery. That's what counseling is all about.

CHAPTER FIVE

DREAM BLOCKS

When I was a high school English teacher, a favorite composition topic that I used to assign to my classes was "If you could be anything in the whole world, without regard to practical factors, like money, time, preparation, and ability, what would you choose to become?" After my students had taken time to think and write down their dreams, we talked about how some of these dreams might come true.

For example, maybe that student from a poor family, who wanted to be a doctor but couldn't afford medical school, could apply for a scholarship. Perhaps the girl who wanted to be a hairstylist but was taking college preparatory classes in order to please her parents should talk to them more directly about her goals and then change to cosmetology. Maybe that boy who wished he were smart enough to be a veterinarian should discover all the related jobs that don't require as much training instead of giving up on working with animals altogether.

Ten years later, as a beginning writer I found myself in the same rut as these students. I hoped someone would want to publish me. Anyone! I found myself thinking that because of my lack of experience as a writer I could approach only lesser-known publishers.

Then one day I remembered those discussions with my students. "Try for the top," I used to say. "You might make it. And if you don't you've lost nothing. All they can say is no."

I found the name of an editor at one of the most respected publishing companies in the country, picked up the phone, and called. By some miracle I got this person immediately. I told her about my book idea and, to my surprise, she said she was interested. Then came the stall, the alert to me that this approach might not work after all. "Send us an outline," she said.

I'll never hear again, I thought. *I should have stuck with the unknowns.*

Teachers since grammar school had been giving me a similar command: "Do an outline; then write your essay." However, I never did outlines. I was the student who wrote the essay, then did the outline, and then turned both of them in, with the teacher never realizing which was done first.

Because the project appeared doomed to failure anyway, I wrote just a one-page summary of the ideas I wanted to expand in my book and mailed it to the editor with little thought of hearing from her again. No positive thinking here! To my surprise, I got a fast answer of acceptance. The publisher actually wanted me.

In my own life I had validated what I had taught my students earlier. "Reach for your dreams and sometimes you realize them. Fail to reach, and you'll never know what you could have done."

To become a dream builder, however, requires a certain basic amount of self-esteem. A good self-image provides much of the raw material for the building blocks with which dreams are built. The dream of building great bridges or organizing large armies or performing delicate surgery; the dream of reaching people through the ideas written on the pages of a book or spoken with power over the airwaves; the dream of a successful marriage and children who are raised with the nurturing of Christian principles—all these are dreams that takes form, in part, because of the sturdy self-esteem that enables them.

Often it starts way back in the early life of a child. Sometimes it begins in a very specific childhood dream. At other times it evolves step by step as the child receives encouragement from a teacher, challenge from a parent, or counsel from a youth pastor. Ideally the growing child not only develops and reaches for dreams but at the same time builds the confidence that will help him or her actually build these dreams.

It is certainly possible to have a low self-image and still be a dream builder, but reaching for the sky is harder when you barely have enough confidence just to survive. Should you actually become a dream builder, maintaining those dreams is harder. The first flash of disapproval or failure can be enough to stop the dream building altogether.

An example of dream building that often comes to my

mind is that of the great founder of the China Inland Mission (now called Overseas Missionary Fellowship). In his early years in China, Hudson Taylor buried his wife and several children in Chinese soil and received severe criticism from both the secular and religious worlds for his insistence on establishing an indigenous church in China. He was ridiculed and resented for his insistence on adapting to Chinese customs of dress and social behavior rather than forcing the Chinese Christians to conform to British customs. These positions received much praise from future generations, but at the time he stood virtually alone.

Dr. Taylor had a dream of opening up the interior of China to the message of Jesus Christ. He was a dream builder. When those dreams, along with his own personal life, seemed to be crashing down around him, he had enough conviction and confidence to go on. Above all, he still believed that the God who had started him on this path would not forsake him.

Others who were not dream builders might have sunk in a mire of doubt. "Maybe this wasn't of God after all," they might reason. "Perhaps I have sinned and God has forsaken me." "God must have another person for the job." "How can I go on when even my Christian brethren do not support me?" Hudson Taylor dared to believe in his God-inspired dream and leaned harder on God with results that can be assessed only in eternity. We know even now, however, that because of a handful of missionaries like him, when Communism took over China in the late forties, Christianity did not die. It grew under the tutelage of adversity.

Most of us are not heroes. Most of us do not aspire to international or even national greatness. However, it is important for all of us to maintain a level of self-esteem that can handle risk taking. In this way we will sometimes attempt the impossible and find that it is indeed very possible. On a more everyday basis, it is important to maintain a certain level of self-esteem just to perform the duties of life.

In spite of their diversity, many of the problems people bring to a counseling office such as mine are based in deficiencies in self-image. Low self-esteem manifests itself in many ways. Bragging is one symptom of a low self-image. If I don't like myself, I may keep telling you how great I am just so that I myself will be convinced. Arrogance is not good self-esteem; it arises from low self-esteem.

Self-denigration is the other extreme. Statements like "I can't do anything right" and "I'm sure they won't like me" are obvious declarations of a low self-image. A sloppy house or careless personal hygiene, as well as overfastidiousness about makeup or clothing or any perfectionism drawn to the extreme, can characterize a person who is down on himself.

More often than not, a person with a low self-image mixes this viewpoint into various aspects of his or her life. There may be insecurity about work but not about relationships. People may be uncomfortable about their appearance but not about their gardens. Some transfer their self-doubt to God and feel that even God can't stand them; others will feel that only God *does* care about them and doubt that anyone else does. Therefore, they may seem to have pockets of low self-esteem and pockets of high self-esteem. The symptoms vary from person to person. In the assessment of self-image, therefore, looking at the whole person is important.

"I don't even go to the doctor anymore," Sam concluded at the end of our first counseling session. "My whole family has died of cancer, and I don't want to know when I get it."

Sam was the proverbial ostrich. In his place of employment he made less money than anyone else because he couldn't bring himself to ask for a raise. Yet when extra time or skill was needed, everyone turned to Sam, who because of his desire to be liked, willingly obliged.

As a child Sam had been unfavorably compared to his older brother. "Why can't you be more like your brother?" was a favorite remark of his mother; his father called him "stupid Sam" when he fell clumsily over his own feet or got a low grade at school.

In later years, even from his deathbed, Sam's father showed his favoritism for Sam's brother. Sam had been at his father's bedside night and day for several days without any show of gratitude from his father for his faithfulness. When Sam's brother cut a lavish vacation short by one day and finally appeared at the hospital, the father gave his older son a warm smile of greeting and said, "I knew you'd come. You always do when I need you."

Actually Sam was a bright, talented young man who, understandably, didn't even know it. "Stupid Sam" stood out in his memory as the only authoritative statement on his life. Only when it was quite obvious that his whole world was using him, and the pain got great enough, did it occur to him that he should get professional help. Through one small glimmer at a time, Sam is beginning to see that he is a sensitive, talented man whom God put on this earth for a specific purpose.

Frequently, a self-image problem is involved even when the presenting symptoms belie the fact. For as long as I have known her, Karen, a woman in her late forties, has been a perpetual victim. Beneath her tendency to feel victimized is a strong sense of inadequacy. In her mind her stepmother resented her; her natural father chose the stepmother over her and thus betrayed her; she has been neglected by her husband; and her boss abuses her willingness to work. Her emotional life cycle resembles a psychological tumbleweed, rolling in the desert sand and picking up more and more dust as it rolls along.

Realistically, Karen has had her share of genuine victimization, particularly as a child. For the most part now, however, she perceives rejection where it doesn't exist. Long ago she disliked herself so intensely that she assumed everyone else disliked her as well. She anticipated rejection where it didn't exist. She became prickly and defensive, so other people reacted in kind, only confirming to her that indeed she was unlikable. Rather than appearing to be vulnerable and insecure, as she truly was, she seemed formidable, even ruthless. Over the years she has convinced herself that she has had a rotten chance at life, and it never seems to occur to her that if *she* changed, her whole world would be different.

However, just as not everyone is like Sam in his determination to face his problems and change, not everyone is like Karen in her determination to blame her environment and to insist that if those around her would just change she could be happy. Some people do know that their self-image problems are hurting their lives, but still they resist the changes in their lives that would be required for them to develop better self-images. They have grown used to hating themselves.

An older couple sat in my office and told of their severe health problems, which their doctor attributed to stress. Moving two adult children, and their spouses, three grandchildren, and one dog into their four-bedroom home with them, so that their children could save money to buy houses, had caused him to leave a thriving law practice and her to seek counseling. Yet what they really were seeking was some miracle answer on how it could all work. "Help us walk on water so we can do all this" was what they wanted from counseling. They did not want to face the insecurity that was driving them to help these adult children they were afraid of losing. They did not want to change. They have dreams that are buried deep inside of them, some of which they have never shared even with each other. But the dream blocks of self-esteem were broken and smashed many years ago. They are no longer dream builders; they just survive, barely.

Some people, however, want to change their lives badly enough to pay the price tag of personal growth. Charlene was a woman in her thirties who came to her first counseling session acutely aware of her self-image problems. "I like helping people," she explained, "but then when their demands increase I just can't say no, and so I feel used. I need to learn to say no regardless of my fear of not being considered nice." Charlene, Sam, and others like them change their lives because they decide to do so, and in so doing they become free to build their dreams, not from something ethereal and unreal but from something set in reality.

Self-esteem is a very vague and often misunderstood term; still it is a pervasive and yet fluctuating factor in every one of our lives. It affects our ability to declare our boundaries and live lives of balance. It influences how effectively we cut all negative tapes. It can make or break our ability to fulfill our God-given dreams. To some it implies a bullish sort of self-worship or arrogance. To others it sounds appealing but unattainable. Still others view good self-esteem as antithetical to faith in God. Yet for those of us in the Judeo-Christian tradition nothing is further from the truth.

The Book of Proverbs balances the issue with perfection: "A man who assists a thief must really *hate himself*! . . ." Compliance in a crime leads only to greater problems; therefore a person with self-respect would not be easily drawn into the self-destructive behavior of a thief. The Book of Proverbs goes on to say: ". . . to *trust* in God means safety" (Prov. 29:24–25 TLB). If self-hate leads only to destruction, the obvious conclusion here is that self-acceptance is a positive factor in good living. Combined with trust in God, it is undefeatable. We must conclude, therefore, that a good self-image is one of the positive building blocks of our human personality, building blocks God uses as long as we remember that both the building blocks and the power to use them are ultimately from Him, not of us.

In the timeless manner in which the Bible is written, a verse in the Book of Romans gives us what I consider the best definition of self-esteem: ". . . not to be thinking more highly of one's self, beyond that which one ought necessarily to be thinking, but to be thinking with a view to a sensible appraisal (of one's self) according as to each one

God divided a measure of faith" (Rom. 12:3, Wuest). Theologian Kenneth Wuest further explains: "All of which goes to say that a Christian should appraise the gifts God has given him fairly, glorifying God for their bestowal, and their exercise through dependence upon the Holy Spirit, and not in mock humility make light of them."[1]

It is a paradox of Christianity that whereas man is in himself totally depraved and cut off from God, in Christ that same man is redeemed and endowed with God-given gifts. Cambridge scholar C. S. Lewis rightly states:

> There are no ordinary people. You have never talked to a mere mortal. Nations, cultures, arts, civilization—these are mortal, and their life is to ours as the life of a gnat. But it is immortals whom we joke with, work with, marry, snub, and exploit—immortal horrors or everlasting splendours. . . . Next to the Blessed Sacrament itself, your neighbor is the holiest object presented to your senses. If he is your Christian neighbor he is holy in almost the same way, for in him also Christ *vere latitat*—the glorifier and the glorified, Glory Himself, is truly hidden.[2]

In the light of God's great value of each human being, we cannot with any sanction from the teachings of Christianity decide that self-hate is Christian. For those who find that conversion to Christ is, in the words of my friend, the late British Bible scholar A. J. Crick, "the moment when I decided that God's will must be mine and I slipped into that wonderful sphere," an honest evaluation of our God-given talents and gifts becomes essential as a starting point in going on to develop and maintain a good self-image. Then, change and growth are in order where sin and imperfection have marred that original perfection that was of God.

It is important, too, to recognize the difference between the vertical and horizontal views of a person's worth.

· Man's relationship to God

Man's relationship to man

An indisputable Christian teaching is that compared to God, man is totally depraved, cut off from God, and in need of redemption, a redemption that is to be found in a personal acceptance of Jesus Christ. Yet God has given great talents, gifts, and qualities of personality for which every person can feel worth. These are dream blocks with which we can each build dreams.

Listening to a sermon preached by my pastor, John Whorrall, I heard a quotation from Phillips Brooks that helped clarify a balanced Christian position on the whole issue of self-esteem: "The true way to be humble is not to stoop until you are smaller than yourself, but to stand at your real height against some higher nature that will show you what the real smallness of your greatness is." In our misguided efforts to be humble we sometimes try to stoop rather than to stand at our real height and grow still higher. We need not fear good self-esteem. God will always be so much higher than we are that knowing that will keep us truly humble.

Just as there is nothing unchristian about a good self-image, there is nothing unchristian about competition. The image of running a race or seeking a prize is a totally biblical concept. If I have a good grasp of intellectual issues, play the piano well, or am a good mother, I can be proud of these qualities. I can further promote my feelings of self-worth by winning a scholarship, entering a painting competition, or enjoying the fact that my children behave better in a restaurant than some others I see. If I have a truly good self-image, I won't need to gloat about these experiences; I'll just enjoy them.

Moreover, the fact that what good qualities we have are gifts from God should not diminish their importance to our sense of self-worth. When I was a small child, my parents gave me a white fur muff and a matching fur hairband for Christmas. The next Sunday morning I went to Sunday school wearing them and feeling very proud indeed. I didn't flaunt them at my friends; I just felt proud of how I looked. They weren't picked out by me, but by my mother; they weren't paid for by me, but by my father. Yet I felt proud because they were now mine. So it is with God's gifts to us. We can be proud of them because He gave them to us, and they are now ours to use in building our lives for His purposes.

Sometimes, however, our dream blocks are marred and crushed. When people cannot see positive qualities in themselves, even when others point them out, counseling can be a safety zone into which they can retreat in order to learn to view themselves more honestly. When people have talents and potentials of which they are aware and yet those abilities lie unused or are used in destructive ways, counseling can help those people develop a better self-image by helping them improve their behavior in those areas.

Thus, growth in the area of self-esteem is two-pronged: recognition of positive God-given talents, gifts, and characteristics and behavioral change in those areas of life that are negative and not worthy of respect. For example, an intelligent student who thinks he is stupid and who fails all his classes may not succeed until he first sees his potential and then works in order to bring his performance up to that potential. Others know they are bright but need simply to study in order to succeed. The first is strictly a self-image problem; the second is a lack of self-discipline that results in low performance and a resultant low self-image.

At times a person who is intellectually capable may not only neglect using that ability for positive purposes, like studying in school, but also compensate for the resultant low self-image by using that same ability for wrongdoing, such as computer theft or vandalism. In summary, to have a good self-image, some people need to see their worth; others need to behave in a more worthwhile way.

Pride is the counterfeit of good self-esteem, and what Kenneth Wuest calls "mock humility" is simply an unchristian condition of self-hate. Either pride or mock humility indicates a sense of low self-esteem and defective dream blocks that make dream building ineffective or even impossible. The Christian teaching that condemns pride and advocates humility can be understood only by a correct definition of these terms, an understanding that is also a basis for good mental health.

To admit to problems of low self-esteem offends the

pride of some people. In a paradoxical way, if we truly do not like ourselves, it is hard to have enough self-confidence to admit to fault. A bluff of "I'm the greatest" or the development of a dictatorial personality may be a cover for the truth, which is "I don't like myself." Periodically I see men who accept the biblical injunction to be heads of their families and forget that they are commanded by the same Bible to love their wives as they love their own bodies. The result is a harsh, dictatorial attitude. They do not have too much ego but too little. Archaic as it may seem, in my years of counseling I have seen more than one man who felt that "spanking" his wife was a form of godly discipline for which he was responsible. I have counseled men who make unreasonable sexual demands and wives who submit because they think it is the Christian way.

Within the marriage relationship, men are certainly not always arrogant in their manifestation of low self-esteem. Often it shows itself in a false humility, a sort of groveling. I can think of one man who values the corner of his garage as his only refuge. For years a dominating wife has degraded him in front of their children and demeaned him before his friends. He has learned that to fight back only makes it worse, so he retreats. In her self-hate, his wife lashes out. Because he does not value himself, he withdraws. Through the years their reactions to each other have only made them hate themselves and each other more. Neither fulfills the biblical role of husband or wife and neither likes the people they have become.

The examples of the destructive, unchristian behavior that can arise from a low self-image are endless. I have counseled women who neglect their children and become the total executive, not because they really want to but because they feel inadequate and are trying to prove that they can do it. They don't appear to have a low self-image, but they do, and that lack of a sense of self-worth drives them to abandon what they really want to do, namely, raise their children.

Then again, many women stay at home for the same reason. These women have talents they want to use in the marketplace, but they don't think they are intelligent enough or clever enough. Self-doubt can cause some people to act when they shouldn't just to prove themselves; for others, self-doubt tends to cripple any constructive action.

Self-love or self-acceptance is not the same as self-worship. Self-worship actually issues forth into the opposite of a good self-image. Self-worship leads to arrogance and self-centeredness, whereas a good self-image enables self-forgetfulness and frees a person to focus on a task or on concern for another human being.

In the words of Kierkegaard:

> If anyone, therefore, will not learn from Christianity to love *himself* in the right way, then neither can he love his neighbor. . . . To love one's self in the right way and to love one's neighbors are absolutely analogous concepts, are at the bottom one and the same. . . . Hence the law is: "You shall love yourself as you love your neighbor when you love him as yourself."[3]

The kind of pride that is to be abhorred by the Christian is a false mock-up of a real self-worth. Pride denigrates the worth of others. Pride does not love. Pride enjoys seeing others fall and will promote itself over the fall of others. Pride always needs to outdo the other person because, underneath, pride is not really very sure of itself at all.

I don't see a lot of pride in my counseling office, but I do see people who are strong enough to seek change and humble enough to ask for it. At times I also see people who are sent by proud people, people who feel too insecure to come themselves because it might mean that something is wrong with them.

Humility is never a state of meek, self-denigrating nothingness. Real martyrs don't enjoy dying; they hate it. Because they are confident people, however, they *dare* to die for what they believe. Real humility takes courage. On an everyday level, humility simply means an absence from self-occupation so that we can attend to our appointed tasks. Humility requires freedom from self, and freedom from self indicates self-confidence. Real humility is, in every sense of the term, a dream block.

C. S. Lewis comments:

> Starting with the doctrine that every individuality is "of infinite value" we then picture God as a kind of employment committee whose business it is to find suitable careers for souls, square holes for square pegs. In fact, however, the value of the individual does not lie in him. He is capable of receiving value. He receives it by union with Christ.[4]

Once received, however, "If God is satisfied with the work the work may be satisfied with itself."[5]

I have noticed that when I do public speaking, which at

times is God's "career" for me, if I am rested physically and confident about what I want to say, I forget myself when I speak. My focus is on the subject matter and on the connection I make between the topic and the audience. I don't worry about how I look, how I sound, or whether I'm succeeding. The task is my focus. Such times of speaking are always successful.

I get into trouble when I am self-conscious. When I focus on myself and how I am coming through, I never do as well. Ironically, self-confidence is a tool that can enable a freedom from thinking about self. Likewise, trusting in God can promote self-confidence, and self-confidence also makes it easier to trust God. The two are mutually supportive, not antithetical.

Furthermore, there is a difference between seeking God's approval and seeking others' approval. There is nothing wrong with liking people's approval of us. In public speaking, for example, when I can see that people are really hearing what I am saying, it is a very rewarding experience and not at all wrong. However, people do not always respond as we wish. Therefore, it is important to look for approval ultimately from God, for only He remains constant.

In talking about heavenly glory and the idea of wanting commendation, Lewis comments about the shock he experienced when he discovered that prominent Christians of the past, like Milton and Thomas Aquinas, interpreted heavenly glory to mean fame, or a good report:

> When I thought it over, I saw that this view was scriptural; nothing can eliminate from the parable the divine accolade, "Well done, thou good and faith-

ful servant." With that a good deal of what I had been thinking all my life fell down like a house of cards. I suddenly remembered that no one can enter heaven except as a child; and nothing is so obvious in a child—not in a conceited child but in a good child—as its great and undisguised pleasure in being praised. Not only in a child, either, but even in a dog or a horse. Apparently what I had mistaken for humility had, all these years, prevented me from understanding what is in fact the humblest, the most childlike, the most creaturely of pleasures—nay, the specific pleasure of the inferior: the pleasure of a beast before men, a child before its father, a pupil before his teacher, a creature before its Creator. . . .[6]

As I was discussing some of these ideas over dinner with a friend, he said in surprise, "But should a Christian seek after success?"

Taken a little aback, because my friend is highly successful in sales, I replied, "How can you ask that? You're very successful yourself."

"I know," he replied, "but I always thought there was something kind of wrong with success. I just do it to survive."

"I just do it to survive." Yet he is doing something in which he obviously excels and even likes. More than that, he is a very fair person who always puts his customer's needs over the sale. That's why people trust him, and that's why he should feel good about this task that God has entrusted to him. Some of our confusions over self-worth and self-hate do not make sense when we really look at them, and they are not very Christian.

Psychologist Rollo May sums up this confusion very well when he says:

> In the circles where self-contempt is preached, it is of course never explained why a person should be so ill-mannered and inconsiderate as to force his company on other people if he finds it so dreary and deadening himself. And furthermore the multitude of contradictions are never adequately explained in a doctrine which advises that we should hate the one self, "I," and love all others, with the obvious expectation that they will love us, hateful creatures that we are; or that the more we hate ourselves, the more we love God who made the mistake, in an off moment, of creating this contemptible creature, "I."[7]

More succinctly, when commenting on a politician who dressed in tattered clothes in order to get the votes of the working man, Socrates exclaimed, "Your vanity shows forth from every hole in your coat."[8]

Some of the worst atrocities in human history have been committed by people who were filled with self-doubt. Adolf Hitler killed six million Jews and five million others in the concentration camps alone. Yet as a child he was sickly, made poor grades in school, and by the time he was fifteen could remember seven changes of address and five different schools. His life passion was to become an artist, a dream that was shattered when he failed to pass the entrance test for the Vienna Academy of Fine Arts. After that, hunger, flophouses, and even jail were his companions until he found the place where he could be somebody—politics. The rest of the story is common know-

ledge, but the beginnings are steeped in self-hate and failure.

Certainly all of the atrocities of World War II, or even
Germany's part in that war, cannot be attributed to Hitler's low self-image or to anyone else's. Economic factors,
the course of history, and the presence of evil itself played
major parts. Nevertheless, the self-hate of this insecure
Austrian provided a major tool for the functioning of that
evil. His own description of his growing hatred of the Jews
is evidence of this: "Gradually I began to hate them," he
commented. "For me this was the time of the greatest
spiritual upheaval I have ever had to go though. I had
ceased to be a *weak-kneed* cosmopolitan and become an
anti-semite."[9]

In his own mind the weak Austrian had now become
strong. Like many others, he mistook pride and, in his
case, even racism for strength instead of the weakness that
it truly was. If he had become truly confident, the world
would have been spared much evil, for then he would not
have felt the need to prove himself in such a pathological
way.

It is important to realize that a good self-image does not
guarantee morality. It does, however, enable the growth
of morality. A good self-image helps a person have the
courage to stand up for what he or she believes. At times
it even helps a person trust in the enablement of God. If
people are too filled with self-doubt, that doubt may keep
them from believing in themselves or in God.

For many the counseling office can become a temporary
safety zone of growth where they can develop a better
sense of self-worth. Psychiatrist Viktor E. Frankl is fond of
a Goethe quote: "If we take man as he is, we make him

worse; if we take him as he ought to be, we help him become it."[10]

Paul Tournier comments: "If one thoughtlessly calls a child a liar, one makes him a liar, in spite of all of his aspirations towards honesty. . . . Call a child stupid, and you make him stupid, incapable of showing what he has it in him to do."[11] What is true of the child is to some extent true of all of us who are adults.

To take people as they ought to be and can become should be the creed of all counseling and psychotherapy. In that atmosphere of acceptance and confrontation, the counseling office becomes a place that fosters growth. It is a place where people assemble the building blocks of self-esteem.

Whether a person develops a good self-image can determine the whole course of a life. In describing a desperate period of his life, the late Sammy Davis, Jr., told an interviewer in 1989, "I didn't like me. So it made all the sense in the world to me at the time that if you don't like yourself you destroy yourself."[12] After such insight and pain, to me it was a tribute to man's God-given potential for growth when Jesse Jackson could say at Mr. Davis's funeral, "He recycled pain into joy."

Counseling is in the business of recycling lives. In the safety zone of the counseling office, many people truly recycle pain into joy, failure into success, futility into meaning, and sorrow into understanding. The end result is dream blocks that can then be used for building dreams. The raw material of these dream blocks is a good self-image.

CHAPTER SIX

DREAM BUILDERS

Somehow Saturday always feels a little less like a work-day to me than the other days I spend in my counseling office. It seems harder to get up in the morning and, like most people, I tend to dress more casually. The routine of being a student and then a teacher dies hard, even after eighteen years. Yet my Saturdays are always busy because that is the best time for anyone who works nine to five to make a weekly counseling appointment.

This particular Saturday was filled with appointments, and I had only a short time off for lunch. Right before I took my noon break, I went into my waiting room and saw a short, rather heavyset man sitting there.

"May I help you?" I inquired.

"You don't know who I am, do you?" the man asked. Then he explained that he was the husband of Susan, a woman I was seeing. Immediately I remembered their situation.

Susan and her husband, Joe, had recently left a small church where they had been members for the last ten years. The church was legalistic and required that all of its members be under the total control of the pastor and the board of elders. Members were not allowed to have any-thing to do with anyone outside the church, even rela-tives; they were obligated to live on a tight budget and hand over all other money to the church; and their chil-dren were educated in a church-controlled private school. Finally, after getting married and having four children, Susan and Joe left the church.

When Susan had first consulted me a few weeks ear-lier, she was undergoing a kind of culture shock. She had no friends; she had a job outside her home for the first time and was afraid of losing it because she was so nervous; and she and Joe were arguing a lot over the rightness of what they had done. Joe wouldn't come in to see me because I was a woman and also because he was afraid that a professional counselor might corrupt his spiritual beliefs.

On this particular Saturday Joe had reached a point of desperation. He had left home early that morning. First he had driven to the beach in hopes of finding a sense of perspective. Next he had called a friend from his former church. The man hung up on him. Then he called his brother who lived across the country. All his brother would say was that he thought Joe had been crazy to go to such a church in the first place. He certainly didn't under-stand any guilt over leaving. Thus, in a state of total des-peration that obliterated any fears he had of being corrupted by me, Joe arrived in my waiting room. "Can you talk to me?" he asked.

The best I could do was give him my lunchtime, which amounted to a tight forty minutes if I let the rest of the day run about ten minutes late. I knew that I had to see him or he might never seek help from anyone again. I realized that in his state of desperation I could not turn him away or make a future appointment. Yet as he started to explain his feelings of guilt and isolation, I felt that we needed a number of sessions, not less than one, to sort out his feelings and start to put the pieces together. It was crisis counseling. I had to make something work *now*.

Within ten minutes I realized that most of the problems he was representing related to the Bible and theology. Did the Bible teach that there was to be a small, select group of Christians who should isolate themselves from other Christians? Did the Bible support the kind of unlove that was shown by the former friend who had just hung up on him that morning? "How can I know that my decision to leave this church was a right one?" he asked.

For the time, I gave up on most psychological solutions and just reinforced his own conclusion that what he was doing had biblical endorsement. He still had God. Here was a man who had been so damaged by so-called Christians that his self-esteem had been shattered. In a very few minutes he received a great deal of help just from being affirmed.

For Joe on that Saturday noon, my counseling office took on all the characteristics of a safety zone. It was secure. It provided refuge from a world that was at that time in Joe's life very hostile. It offered a place of recovery from a very shattering experience. It was available for his needs.

Over the next few weeks the rebuilding came quickly. Even the psychological repair of the damage to his confidence required only a few sessions. Mainly, in his case, all he needed to know was what any Christian with a basic knowledge of the Bible could have pointed out to him. He and God were okay in their relationship.

Susan and Joe both needed a short period of support and some suggestions on the practical rebuilding of their lives and those of their family. They needed friends, a new church, schools, and a whole way of life that they had almost forgotten existed. Counseling also helped Joe and Susan to keep the Christian beliefs that were so vital to them while they shed the extreme teaching of the group with whom they had been associated for ten years. (In years to come, the help they received in those few weeks of counseling enabled them to assist others who left the same church group and who, like them, felt desolate and guilt-ridden.)

After having their dream blocks crushed and broken for years, Joe and Susan once again became dream builders. Once her confidence reached a certain level, Susan went back to teaching, a profession she had dropped at the church's orders. Joe redeveloped a hobby of cabinetmaking and eventually helped delinquent boys by teaching them this skill. Both of them had raised their self-images through counseling. Then, as they developed their lives and succeeded, that self-esteem increased even more.

Each of us has dreams. Sometimes those dreams are so hidden within us that we are barely aware of them. Along the way people may have made us believe that only the young have dreams or, worse still, that it is wrong to dream at all. But even if we are aware of our dreams, if we have too much self-doubt, or if we have not developed some skills that enable us to handle relationships with friends in the present and memories of the past, we will find ourselves forgetting our dreams and lowering our expectations of life to simple survival.

Self-esteem is a basic material in dream blocks, but self-esteem can be elusive. It is vital to good mental health, and yet it can be fragile and fluctuating. Paradoxically, it can be sturdy, too. It never ceases to amaze me how fast a damaged self-image can be restored and how quickly it can be once again dashed to the ground. In the case of Joe and Susan, for example, once they left their church, they felt, understandably, guilty and relieved at the same time. Then they met with blatant rejection from all their friends, which in turn made them feel more guilty. Their children were upset, which increased their sense of guilt.

For a while they didn't know whether to feel guilty for having been part of such a church or guilty because they had left. This frustration further lowered their self-images. The vicious circle went on. Every change, rejection, failure, and sharp word of criticism just intensified the downward spiral of their self-esteem. Even God seemed to be rejecting them!

For Joe and Sue, counseling provided a safety zone of support and growth that reversed the process. Because we were all of the Christian faith, I was able to reinforce them spiritually as well as psychologically. Had they been Jewish, for example, and had their problems been related to their Jewish faith, I might have needed the help of a rabbi. With Joe and Sue, spiritual support started the reversal of the downward spiral of their self-esteem, so that it now began to spiral up. After that beginning, each friend they added to their lives, each success, each insight they gained into their own God-given gifts and talents, each kind word, each tool for living, all these continued that spiral upward until Joe and Susan were ready to continue their growth without the safety zone of counseling. They had learned skills and been given tools that enabled them to rebuild the raw material of their lives, the dream blocks of self-esteem. Once again they became dream builders.

Most of the people I counsel do not present the same magnitude of spiritual problems that Joe and Susan had. Still, sometimes the lines between people's spiritual needs, emotional problems, physical ailments, and even something as simple as the need for friendship are very hard to distinguish.

In his insightful book *The Doctor and the Soul,* Viktor E. Frankl portrays the unique problems of those who seek the refuge of the counseling office for problems that are more specifically spiritual than psychological:

> People are constantly coming to us with problems such as, what is the meaning of their lives. . . . Medicine, and psychiatry in particular, has thereby been compelled to cope with a new field. . . . Medical ministry [or, I might add, counseling ministry] does not aspire to be a substitute for the proper cure of souls which is practiced by the minister or priest.[1]

In essence, people today have tremendous problems with meaning. These problems pervade their feelings about their personal worth, their dealings with suffering, and their sense of values. Yet in the middle of a spiritual desert, there is a tendency to seek out the psychiatrist, the psychologist, or the counselor rather than the priest, the minister, or the rabbi.

To me the reason lies primarily in the definition of the counseling office as a safety zone. The other day a patient said to me, "When I went to my pastor, he condemned me and told me I was sinning and not being a good wife. Thank you for not doing that."

In actuality, the woman is a "good" wife and a "good" woman. She and her husband even have a fairly stable relationship. However, her self-esteem problems make her overly sensitive to his criticism, an oversensitivity that was not improved by the condemnation and harshness she received from her pastor. Quietly, she simply left the church and sought professional help.

If her pastor had viewed his counseling office as a place to build people up, as well as a place of confrontation if that was required, and if that confrontation had been done in love, then she might not ever have left his church. Furthermore, had he been willing, any professional counseling could have been done with the support of the pastor's spiritual counsel. Dream blocks of self-esteem would have been built rather than destroyed.

Paul Tournier, who is a solid Christian as well as a psychiatrist, makes what is to me a sad comment on the subject of the relationship of many who seek professional counseling and the church to which they belong. In speaking of the counseling office as a place, Dr. Tournier says:

> Through us and our place, the patient is attached once more to society, and often also to God and the Church, which then become for him the best possible

place. Nevertheless I ought to say that it is often very difficult for a patient who has been cured, or at least undergone an improvement in his condition, to feel at home in the Church, even if he wants to. He finds it so impersonal, so cold and conventional, after the stirring experiences he has had in the psychotherapist's consulting room.[2]

This should not be, for divine love, lived out through God's people, should surpass the human love found in any counseling office.

In the parable of the prodigal son, his sin, and his subsequent return to his father's house, there is repentance of sin, but there is no further reproach, no period of probation, no "I told you so." Yet no one, including the prodigal son himself, denied that the basis of his problems had been sin. He had caused his own problems.

Most people who seek psychological counseling, however, have not caused their own problems by blatant wrongdoing. They just hurt. Certainly their welcome from the church should be as warm as that given to the prodigal son. Above all other places, the church and the pastor's consulting room should be places of affirmation and safety. Affirmation is one function of the safety zone of counseling. Affirmation builds people; affirmation reverses the downward cycle of low self-esteem.

Recently, someone said to me in a careless afterthought, "You know, if I wanted to be sure that others understood of my pain, I'd probably pick a bar to go to rather than a church. At least I wouldn't be criticized."

There is nothing so comforting on this earth as the love of God poured out to us from Christians who are filled with God's love. But when that love is absent, Christian standards can begin to feel harsh indeed. If some seek comfort in bars instead of in Christian fellowship, then we who are Christians need to examine the quality of our love.

This in no way implies that we must lower our standards of what is right and wrong. But it does mean that we allow God to love other people through us, whether or not they agree with us. To love the unlovely, to love the unresponsive: this is the truest test of the reality of our love.

Consistent with this way of thinking, just because we disagree with someone, or even when we feel they are morally wrong, does not excuse unlove or poor manners. In the words of Amy Carmichel, " . . . if anyone is inclined to think that rudeness and honesty run together, and politeness and insincerity, I will tell you what I have found: The strongest, bravest, truest people I ever knew were (are) the most gentle-mannered. Good manners are not among the things that do not matter. Can we imagine our Lord Jesus ever being rude?"[3]

God is our ultimate Affirmer. He made us in His image and redeemed us with His blood. His affirmation alone imputes great value to the worth of each individual human being. In the words of Helmut Thielicke, "For God does not love us because we are so valuable; rather we are valuable because God loves us."[4]

God's view of man, furthermore, places a strong obligation upon the members of His church to become affirmers. Read any of the greetings from Paul to members of the early church, for example, and you will find commendation and praise of a whole host of people. Surrounded by

active persecution, these people needed each other's affirmation if they were to continue building the church in the
middle of such great trouble. Providing a theological basis
for such affirmation, Thielicke continues, "Because the
other person is valuable to God he compels me to show
reverence. Therefore my love is no longer addressed to an
unstable function, to what in any given moment I can or
cannot find to be 'valuable for me' in the other person."[5]

In describing the affirming atmosphere of a large hospital in Germany, Paul Tournier adds to our understanding of the practical potential of affirmation from even just
one individual when he quotes its head physician as
saying:

> I think I can say that my hospital is pervaded by a
> personal spirit, but I believe we owe this almost en-
> tirely to a single person—our Sister Superior, who is
> so profoundly human that everyone whose life she
> touches feels that he is considered a person, feels
> himself becoming a person.[6]

That each human being is valuable is basic to any counseling that sets out to help rebuild lives. When affirmation
from friends is not enough to restore a damaged self-
image, or when that affirmation is not forthcoming, then it
becomes the province of the professional counselor.

Affirmation must be based on truth, however, or it
builds upon a very shaky foundation indeed. Furthermore, affirmation is usually a simple process that may
involve sorting out facts, evaluating situations, and simply
telling someone that he or she is okay.

Not long ago a man in his early thirties told me in poignant detail how he used to come home from school and ask his mother, "What is wrong with me? Why do the other kids tease me?"

Today John is handsome, a successful architect, and happily married. Yet underneath all that success he harbored a nagging feeling that he was not worthwhile. He sought counseling and asked me the same question he had asked his mother years earlier, "What is wrong with me?"

Together we figured out that because John had been a small, shy boy who was bad at sports but exceptionally good academically, he stood out and became the perfect victim. Then, because no one ever taught him how to deal with teasing, he responded in all the wrong ways. He lost his temper, cried, and hid from his tormentors. These reactions just fueled more teasing. After all, a bully always enjoys a victim who reacts.

As John began to realize why he had been teased and saw that when he was a child there had been no relationship between his real worth and what he considered then to be his unpopularity, he was free to evaluate himself more honestly in the present. He learned to value strengths, like his creativity as an architect, the respect of his friends, his faithfulness to his children, and the love of a good wife. Ironically, he grew closer to God, too. That deep gut feeling that no one could really like him, including God, had almost disappeared. John was free enough from self-occupation to grow and to reach out to others. Paradoxically, because he liked himself more, he thought of himself less. He didn't have to worry about whether he was okay.

People who have low self-images may not be able to see

the truth about themselves, even when all the facts are obvious. At such a point the pastor, the friend, or the professional counselor is needed to help these people see themselves more clearly. A woman who was a very competent teacher consulted me because of a number of relationships that all seemed to be going badly. On the surface there were at least two possibilities: either Brenda was offending people and didn't wear well in long-term friendships or she was choosing the wrong people as friends. Some of the differences between her and two of her friends revolved around money.

Brenda had borrowed two thousand dollars from a friend in order to buy a car for transportation to her first teaching job. The friend asked her to pay a hundred a month, then two hundred, then two hundred fifty. The escalating payments were seriously restricting Brenda in other areas. Other bills went unpaid. Messages from bill collectors began to appear on her answering machine. Thoughts of what she owed kept her awake at night. She could no longer afford dinner with friends, which made her feel isolated. Compounding her anxiety, the friend's demands to keep paying more persisted and worried her. Then, when she could least afford it, counseling became a necessity because of all the anxiety.

We began by talking about possible sources of additional income. Then I asked her how much longer the payments would continue. "My friend says that if I go to four hundred a month I'll be paid up in four more months," she replied.

When she said this, my mind blurred, and yet momentarily I went along with her thinking: four months would be tough, but she should focus beyond four months to the day when her debt would be paid and she would be free of that particular pressure. Then, suddenly, it all became clear to me. Brenda hadn't even kept track of her payments. She had just trusted her friend's word. In truth, she had already overpaid the debt she owed. In four months, at four hundred dollars a month, her friend would have owed Brenda more than two thousand dollars! Brenda reacted with relief first and then anger. "I just assumed that she was right and I was wrong," she said.

In an ironic sort of role reversal, she then explained that her other close friend, also a teacher, owed *her* five hundred dollars. The friend had recently called to ask how much Brenda wanted her to pay each month. The friend even suggested fifty dollars a month. Brenda's question to me was a hesitant "Do you think I could dare to ask her for fifty dollars a month?"

Brenda is a good example of a person who is honest and tries to be a good friend. Because she doesn't respect herself, she chooses people who take advantage of her. She doesn't see this, however, and assumes that the resultant problems have to be her fault. She doesn't trust herself enough to feel that she could be right. For her, counseling needs to help her evaluate her worth more honestly and see the value she has and, once that is accomplished, to encourage her to improve her choice of friends. As this occurs, the building blocks of self-esteem will be formed, and she will be free enough from herself to build her dreams.

Affirmation, whether it becomes part of the counseling

process or remains in the province of friendship, is simply reinforcement of the fact that God doesn't make junk. The late Walter Trobisch made a great contribution in his writings on self-esteem. In *Love Yourself*, Trobisch drew from his missionary background to give a clear example in the area of self-esteem and affirmation:

> When I write this I have to think of my African friends. It seems so much easier for them to accept themselves than for us Westerners. I am reminded of one of my best friends, an African man who is rather short. A well-meaning person once suggested to him that he wear shoes with higher heels in order to appear taller.
>
> This was almost an offense to my friend. Hadn't God made him short? Why should he seek to change what God had created? He had accepted himself as he was and loved himself with his height. I am sure this complete self acceptance is one of the reasons that he can be such a good friend to me.[7]

Although a change in self-perception is one aspect of changing one's self-image, often a change in behavior is required also. Brenda, the teacher who owed her friend money, for example, needed to change her perception of her own worth as well as change her way of dealing with both her use of money and her choice of friends. She needed to realize that she was worth having healthy friends. One symptom of low self-esteem is that very capable, worthwhile people sometimes choose irresponsible friends. They feel that no one they respect would want to be their friend, or they feel that by choosing unstable friends they don't have to feel threatened and can even feel superior.

For those who feel that most of their friendships are unsatisfactory, it is important to ask, Do I choose people who always fail me because I feel unworthy of more reliable friends? Are these the only people who will be my friends because I don't give much back in a friendship? If the answer to the former is yes, you may need a whole set of new friends, and the problems in your friendships may relate more to the kinds of people you associate with rather than your failure as a friend. If the answer to the latter question is yes, you need to learn to be a better friend yourself. In either case, whether you choose poorly or behave poorly, self-esteem is probably a major factor. One thing I am sure of is that most people choose friends who basically share the same level of mental health.

For this reason it is wise to make sure that one's self-image is secure before making major life decisions, such as choosing a life partner. As I said to one patient, "Six months ago you would have chosen a fairly damaged individual. Today you would make a better choice. Six months from now, you will probably choose a partner with whom you truly want to spend the rest of your life."

Sometimes changing a person's self-image means going beyond just choosing better friends or dealing more efficiently with life. It can mean facing wrongdoing. According to Martin Luther, to *repent* is to do so no more. That is the best definition I've ever heard, and it works. The businessman who came to me who was sleeping with his wife's best friend and was fraudulent in his business practices also didn't like himself. At first he thought that counseling was supposed to make him realize that he was really a fine man, regardless of his behavior. "You're supposed to make me like myself," he said to me. The problem was that he wasn't a fine man!

Certainly he had some good qualities of personality and a keen business sense. He knew that without any help from me. Because of the moral fiber of his life-style, however, his self-esteem could never be strong without massive changes in his behavior. From just a practical point of view, if he continued in his present direction, he could look forward to the destruction of his marriage, his family, and his business and perhaps to a change of address (to jail!).

To have simply developed an honest perception of himself would have lowered his self-image more than it would have raised it. Forgiveness and change had to be the basis for a better self-image. Any psychological mind trip that attempts to make a person feel good about doing bad is not sound either psychologically or spiritually, and it doesn't work on any long-term basis.

Sometimes, however, the need to change is not based upon dealing with wrongdoing as much as it involves certain changes in behavior that just work better. Although procrastination, lack of organization, untidiness, shyness, and many other similar characteristics may have nothing to do with sin, they often demand change if a person's self-image is to improve. These qualities are not wrong in themselves, but they often make people feel bad about themselves. Shyness can isolate us, untidiness can keep us from hospitality or make us feel inadequate when we do entertain, and procrastination can make us lose jobs or alienate us from friends.

Christianity provides the solution to issues involving

sin, but Christians are often the least understanding in areas that relate to imperfection. In our confusion, we tend to merge the two and thus develop the "confess your depression" brand of counseling that ends up being destructive to so many.

C. S. Lewis gives the best example I have seen of the difference between those things in our personality that are simply imperfect and yet still affect our self-image and those ways of behavior that lower our self-image because they are sinful.

In his book *Mere Christianity* Lewis gives an apt illustration of the difference between situations that involve human frailty and those that require moral choice. Three men go to war. One has a certain fear of the danger involved, but he rises above that fear and shows courage. The other two have such great fears regarding war that they cannot fight. Their fears go beyond the rational to the irrational. Moral choice alone cannot conquer the fears. At that point a psychoanalyst treats the two and cures them. The psychological problem ends and the moral problem starts. Now that they are cured, they can respond with relief but still refuse to make the choice to fight. On the other hand, now that they are cured, they can make the choice to go ahead and do what is right.

Says Lewis, "The bad psychological material is not a sin but a disease. It does not have to be repented of, but to be cured. . . . Human beings judge one another by their external actions. God judges them by their moral choices."[8]

To summarize, again in the words of Lewis, "Fear is horrid but there's no reason to be ashamed of it. Our Lord was afraid of Gethsemane."[9] But our Lord never sinned.

I once saw an eleven-year-old boy who seemed to be having problems in every area of his life. His family couldn't get along with him, he fought with his classmates, and his grades had fallen dramatically from the previous year. After a few sessions that clearly pointed out his lack of self-confidence but didn't give a clue as to its source, I asked what proved to be the vital question, "Why do you always wear a baseball cap?"

In typical preteen fashion he mumbled, "I don't know."

"Would you care to take it off for just a moment?" I asked.

After considerable persuasion, Justin took off his cap, and I knew why he wore the cap. Without the cap Justin's hair stood straight up! He quickly replaced the hat and told me that for the past year he had refused to take it off for just that reason. His hair stood up, and everyone teased him. Teasing for *wearing* the cap was less painful. For one year Justin's grades and social relationships had plummeted because of his hair. Justin wanted to be a doctor. With his current academic progress that goal was becoming unattainable. He had stopped building toward his dreams.

Justin's mother either cut Justin's hair herself or sent him to the cheapest barber she could find. I suggested someone more qualified, in lieu of paying even more to me for additional counseling. She agreed. The next and last time I saw Justin he was happy and relaxed. All his self-esteem needed was a good haircut!

It was important, too, for Justin himself to be willing to take off his cap and tell about being teased—and not to be forced to do either. Even the smallest child should feel a sense of privacy about his or her inner thoughts. Only where major issues are involved, like drugs or physical danger, should the adult world forcibly intrude. In this way the child retains the right to be a person. The child grows up with a sense of self-respect.

As a small child of about five, I remember feeling intimidated one afternoon when my mother asked me questions about my relationship with God. I didn't disagree with her beliefs. Very early in life I had turned my life over to Jesus Christ. I was definitely a Christian. Nevertheless, I remember so clearly standing in the dining room and thinking, *They can make me do whatever they want. But they can't look into my mind. My thoughts are my own.* It was undoubtedly my way of asserting myself as a person, separate from my parents, even if I did agree with them. It was my way of having a private world in the sometimes not so private world of a child.

In order to develop and maintain a good self-image, every human being, regardless of age, has to maintain feelings of dignity. To help people do that is to be an affirmer. For example, just because someone who is aged may be physically helpless does not mean that his or her private life should be openly discussed without regard for their feelings. Children too old to be undressed in front of other people, and too young to protest, should have their needs attended to in private. Criticism of employees, the clarification of a problem with a friend, and confrontation in general should never be done in the presence of people who are not involved in the problem.

The counseling office, above all other places, should

always be a place of dignity and safety. Especially in this place of rebuilding and growth, each individual should feel the right to reveal himself at his own pace. No one should feel intimidated to tell more than he can or foolish if he cannot at first feel complete trust. Trust is earned, especially the trust that must eventually exist between the counselor and the counselee in this very intimate human relationship.

I remember a teenage girl who was sent to me by a social worker so that I could determine her needs in terms of foster care and adoption. She had been brutally molested for a number of years. When she walked into my office, she said, "I've already told the police what happened. I don't want to talk about it again." I agreed, and we talked about where she wanted to live and what she wanted to do with her life.

Halfway through the hour she asked, "Do you mind if I tell you what happened? I'd like you to know." When she told me what were probably the most intimate details of her life so far, it was her decision to share them with me; it was her act of trust. She had been allowed the dignity of choice. The safety zone of counseling had not been just a place where she found solutions to her problems; it had been a place where her self-image was reinforced by providing an atmosphere of respect for her as an individual.

Not every self-image problem is deep-seated or deals with wrongdoing. In the marriage counseling I do, I have often thought many marital problems would never develop if the husband would occasionally take care of the baby in the evening while his wife went shopping, or if the wife would encourage her husband to take time out to do something relaxing for a few minutes after he gets home from work. A cold drink served to someone who is working outside in the heat, a thank-you for a task well done, a few minutes of time spent listening, even when you don't feel like it—such trivia make up the fabric of domestic life; and both giving and receiving such seemingly small acts of consideration elevate a person's sense of self-worth.

If rebuilding a damaged self-image in the privacy of a counseling office teaches us anything about technique, it teaches us that self-confidence is most effectively learned through receiving the understanding of another human being and giving love to others around us. Then the more I like this person called *me*, the more I am free from focusing on me. A person who has a strong self-image doesn't have to always prove that he or she is right. A person with a strong self-image doesn't have to be afraid to say, "I'm sorry."

An effective counselor sees the patient for all of his or her potential. An attractive young woman walked into my office last week and gave a highly intelligent explanation of why she was seeking counseling. What I saw and heard was intelligent, attractive, and well-mannered. Yet she summarized her needs by describing herself as stupid and ugly. When her perception of herself more closely resembles that of those who know her, she will no longer need counseling. She will have acquired sound building material with which to develop her life.

G. K. Chesterton once wrote of Saint Francis:

He deliberately did not see the mob for the men. . . . He only saw the image of God multiplied but never monotonous. To him a man was always a man and did not disappear in a dense crowd any more than in a desert. He honoured all men; that is he not only loved but respected them all . . . there was never a man who looked into those brown burning eyes without being certain that Francis Bernardone was really interested in him; in his own inner individual life from the cradle to the grave; that he himself was being valued and taken seriously. . . . [10]

In my bedroom I have large floor-to-ceiling windows. Through these windows I can look out and see the mountains in the distance and the trees that line my street. Across the street are two particularly beautiful trees that, unlike so many trees in California, change with the seasons. A few years ago the man who lived across the street decided to put a low wall across the front of his yard. He brought in a supply of bricks and mixed some mortar. At first bricks were spread all around. Then he began, brick by brick, to build the wall.

At first, all it amounted to was one row of bricks cemented together, and then another row just like it. The whole process took several days, brick by brick. After a while a pattern began to emerge. This was not going to be an ordinary brick wall, after all. The bricks began to be staggered rather than just set evenly on top of each other until, at the end, a very artistic brick wall surrounded the walkway and the two beautiful trees.

Dream builders do something very similar with their lives. First they have a dream. Then they build with dream blocks. Sometimes the dream blocks become damaged and need to be repaired. Often they need to be reinforced. Whatever the cost, for the dream builders, the building goes on. Then, someday before they know it, the form of something far more wonderful than they imagined may emerge. The dream will have become concrete.

CHAPTER SEVEN

THE GOD CONNECTION

Mr. Sam Eddie," the receptionist called out into the hospital waiting room, which was full of people waiting to have their blood drawn, hopefully soon so that they could go home.

An elderly man across from me rose to his feet with that look of hesitancy that so often accompanies a feeling of not being sure whether your name or that of someone else was called.

"Mr. Sam Eddie?" the receptionist inquired of the man as he approached her.

"Oh no," he fumbled. "I'm Freddie Brown."

The receptionist smiled with that patronizing look people sometimes get around the elderly when they conclude that age has made a person incompetent. Assuming the tone of voice and facial expression of one speaking to a small child, she replied, "Don't worry. We'll get to you soon."

With a look of awkward embarrassment, Mr. Freddie Brown returned to his seat and sat down. He rubbed his face nervously and glanced quickly around to see how many people had observed his faux pas.

Not long afterwards the receptionist called out another name. "Melissa Smith, please come to the desk."

No one moved. To one side of the room two teenage girls sat chatting. After the second call for Melissa Smith, one girl nudged the other and said laughingly, "Pay attention, that's you!" The receptionist smiled, and no one turned to look.

A man in his eighties wasn't sure that it was his name that was called. A teenager didn't even hear her name or any other name called! In terms of confusion or lack of accuracy of hearing, the teenager was the worst offender. The assumption of senility for the older man arose from the apparent age of the individual, not from the symptoms he presented.

It's a principle of living that we each have a lot to do with what other people become, for they tend to become what we expect them to become. In no two periods of life is this concept more aptly portrayed than in childhood and again in old age. I have seen children denigrated, with the result that they grew up feeling worthless. Conversely, I have seen children praised and encouraged until they actually achieved far more than anyone ever thought possible.

A little boy who had been in many foster homes was finally adopted. His first teacher in the school near his new home praised him almost too much, I thought. Yet because of her encouragement, he worked hard in her class and started to catch up on the years of school he had lost. Then his adopted family moved and he started at a new school. "You're going to end up in jail someday," the teacher shouted at him in anger when the child disturbed her class for the third time in one day. After a few similar statements, his behavior grew steadily worse. One day he stole from a grocery store. His comment to me afterwards was, "I might as well steal; that's what everyone expects me to do!"

At least children can look forward to the day when they will have more complete control of their destinies and when their value to society will exceed that of tax deductions for their parents. For the elderly, there is no such hope. If their present is dismal, their hope for the future is darker still. Rather than old age being a time of honor, as in the older Chinese culture, or a time of spiritual leadership and even reward, which is part of the Judeo-Christian heritage, age has become to our present society the disease of our time. We predestine ourselves and others to a dread of old age, and in some kind of self-fulfilling prophecy it truly becomes, in many instances, a terrible time.

Certain aspects of aging can be dreadful. Brittle bones, poverty, loss of memory, and helplessness are at times realistic expectations. For those who are the relatives or friends of the elderly person thus afflicted, it is often difficult to know what to do. It is important to realize, however, that our own attitudes toward aging and the aged tend to influence how well the elderly handle their lives. As often as not, negative expectations of the elderly do them as much harm as the actual afflictions themselves. Furthermore, the kinds of perceptions we have regarding old age will help to determine not only our treatment of the elderly but also our own gradual but consistent aging process.

When my mother died of injuries sustained in a car accident, she was almost eighty years old. For eleven days after the accident, she fought to live. At the scene of the accident, she was clearer than anyone else regarding the practical details, such as who was in the car and where they lived. For seven years after the death of my father, she had lived in their house by herself. She gardened, baked, took care of two dogs, painted some of her best work, and was, in general, an active participant in life. Above all, she was fun. She could always be ready at a moment's notice to go out for a late supper or to take a ride by the ocean.

Yet one of the doctors who didn't know her and, indeed, had never met her before the surgery that followed the accident—and who ironically was elderly and white-haired himself—greeted me with the question, "Which convalescent home was she in?"

When I replied that she had never been in a convalescent home, the doctor responded, "Anyone who is eighty should be in a convalescent home!"

His opinion is a perfect illustration of the idiotic preconceptions that sometimes plague the elderly. Unfortunately, when the elderly themselves hear such statements, they sometimes begin to feel that maybe, after all, they are useless. They can begin to become what they hear others saying about them.

Furthermore, for those of us who deal with aging loved ones or help others work with them, it is important that we not only deal with our own fears of growing old but also clarify within our own minds our view of the meaning of old age.

After centuries of seeking the fountain of youth, we

have now doubled our life expectancy. But what is the value of these added years? Sorting out our values on aging, including our own aging, can be a function of the safety zone of counseling. If we view old age as throw-away years, we make it hard for the aged to find meaning in those years, and we make it very difficult for ourselves as caretakers of the aged. Time so spent will seem wasted and difficult.

It had been an unusual day in my office. After a number of years of listening to people, not many problems shock or upset me in the sense that they profoundly disturb my personal life. In my office I am totally involved in my patients' problems, but when I leave that office, I cut the tapes of that day. This day was different.

The child I had seen was only seven, but she had endured months of brutal sexual molestation from an uncle who seemed, to all outward appearances, totally normal. Something like this is always hard to deal with emotionally. Still, I have seen numbers of children who have been either physically abused or sexually molested. Some have been much younger than seven. Perhaps it was the frequency of the acts against this child that horrified me; perhaps it was the fact that for so long no one had listened to her or defended her that bothered me so much. Perhaps it was the attitude of the uncle, who regretted what he had done but, by his own admission, would have gone out and done the same thing again if it had been possible. Perhaps it was the volume of details I heard, not only from the child, who was hesitant, but also from the uncle himself, who seemed unable to resist enjoying his recital of lurid details.

I came home that night feeling physically sick to my

stomach. It was one of those times when I felt that only the purity of God Himself could cleanse me from what I had heard and help me put it from my mind. I felt alone, and so I picked up the phone and called a friend, the mother of a childhood schoolmate of mine.

My friend is elderly. She is not in wonderful health. She is a godly woman who has probably not ever heard anything quite like what I heard in my office that day. Nevertheless, I knew she would understand, and she did. As we talked, I felt that sense of godly authority from her that is so characteristic of those who have walked with God for many years. The nausea left, and I was able to cut the tapes and commit the child to God.

I was reminded again of the challenges in the New Testament for older women to counsel those who are younger. I thought, too, of the verses that warn against one Christian saying to another, in essence, "I don't need you." We all need each other, the aged and the young alike.

> From childhood I am inspired with wonder;
> From adolescence I am challenged to question and search;
> From adulthood I am inspired by ambition and work;
> From old age, I discover reward, contemplation and sharing.

By sharing between different age groups, those who are older retain the good of the age they have outgrown while those who are younger share the benefits of those who are ahead of them in time. Those who are not yet aged cannot afford to say to the aged, "I don't need you." We need them very much, and they need us.

In our society retirement often becomes a signpost marking the end of productivity and the beginning of the great slide downhill toward death. The gift of a watch at that time is appropriate as a symbol of the last countdown. Often the retiree tries to deny the inevitable, for a while at least, by a burst of activity; others slump into a hopeless resignation to the inevitable from which they never completely recover.

Although old age marks the latter end of life, that fact does not contradict the equally true fact that old age can be a time of great meaning. Those years are not throwaway years. Otherwise God, who holds all time in His hands, would certainly remove all old people from the earth, for He does not leave any of us here without a purpose. Indeed, in the thoughts of the psalmist, God has scheduled each day of our lives before we begin to breathe. Each day has value.

Charles Spurgeon has aptly stated, "Old age is a time of peculiar memories, of peculiar hopes, of peculiar solicitudes, of peculiar blessedness, and of peculiar duties." [1] Arguing against those who view aging as a time of defeat, General Douglas MacArthur is quoted as saying:

> People grow old only by deserting their ideals. . . . Years may wrinkle the skin, but to give up interest wrinkles the soul. . . . You are as young as your faith, as old as your doubt; as young as your self-confidence, as old as your fear; as young as your hope, as old as your despair. In the central place of every heart there is a recording chamber; so long as it receives messages of beauty, hope, cheer and courage, so long are you young. When . . . your heart is

covered with the snows of pessimism and the ice of
cynicism, then and only then are you grown old.[2]

The general would have agreed, I believe, that we can
measure our age by the tapes we play.

As we begin to see those we love grow older and at
times become increasingly helpless, however, it is natural
to question the value of life at that point. We read the
words of English poet Robert Browning, "The best is yet
to be," and we wonder how. Yet even at its extremity,
there is meaning in a life that on the surface may look
meaningless.

A man of around eighty sat in my office telling me of his
wife to whom he had been married some fifty years. She
had developed Alzheimer's diesase and required total
care, which this man was trying to give her at home. When
I asked him why he didn't put her in a convalescent home,
a gentle look came over his face.

"Sometimes I don't know why," he started to explain,
"but at night when she's asleep lying in bed next to me,
she's herself again. I hold her, and look at her; and I have
my wife again for just a little while."

A short while later the woman died suddenly of a heart
attack. By the time she died, her husband had become
accustomed to doing without her. During that long transition between earth and Heaven, however, unknown to
her until eternity, she had been a comfort to her grieving
husband. She had helped him get used to her dying. Even
with the worst symptoms of her disease, her life had been
meaningful.

When old age is ravaged by a disease like Alzheimer's,
however, counseling has to provide support for the care-

takers involved. Balance in considering each person's needs is necessary. Every living being deserves dignity; a person who needs total care still deserves privacy, gentleness, and compassion. However, the caretakers also deserve consideration in the sense of encouragement in knowing how far they should be directly involved in caring for their elderly loved ones. Providing a sounding board in order to determine those boundaries, helping caretakers declare those boundaries to other family members, and then helping them cut the tapes of guilt, which often exist regardless of how much they are doing, can be a valuable service.

It is popular in the times in which we live to declare our independence of the elderly or the handicapped. We don't want anything to clutter up our neatly planned lives. Yet in the end such selfishness breeds emptiness and even exacerbates our own fears of who will be there for us when we are the aged. Most of us realize that as we treat the aged in our lives, so will our children learn to treat us.

For all they did for us in raising us and influencing us when we were young, the elderly deserve care in their old age. On a higher level still, for those of us who claim to be Christians and as such are obligated to live up to a very high standard of love, it is a biblical principle that we are to help those who are helpless and need our care. In those families where there was abuse or neglect in childhood, there is the greater challenge of Christian love that returns good for evil.

However, caretakers who are driven by guilt to become self-made martyrs help no one. It is wise to take breaks and to know one's limitations in caretaking.

After my mother's death, my Aunt Lydia was also close

to death. For days we did not even tell her of my mother's death. When at last she was stabilized, she was released from the hospital to a convalescent home for two or three weeks of further recovery. It was a chance for those of us who had been responsible for her care to have a brief respite. I remember feeling some guilt over leaving her for what ended up as a long weekend. But a sense of perspective won out. By leaving town for a much-needed change, we would be better equipped in the long run to take care of her. A vacation was good economy. Of course, my aunt would rather have had us stay, but she understood.

For many of the aged, however, practical usefulness, the ability to perform a task, is certainly not necessarily obliterated by the passage of time. Old age is not always debilitating. The book *Our Aging Society* reminds us of the increase in life expectancy that has occurred since the beginning of this century, when the average person lived only forty-seven years. Now, as we approach the end of the nineteen hundreds, sixty-five is too soon for most people to retire, much less die.

The authors speak of the third quarter of life, the period between fifty and seventy-five, as a time of active productivity.[3] To those of us who deal with the elderly, and who are in that middle period ourselves, the concept of the third quarter should be an encouraging signpost—fifty is no longer over the hill—even if you consider active productivity to be the only form of meaning in this world.

The concept of the third quarter has been more than validated in my experience. I have seen people who are even *beyond* that third-quarter mark and yet are as active as the general population: a psychiatrist in his late seventies who still practices in spite of poor health and whose advice is as clear and sharp as ever; a pastor whose insights into the Scriptures have only deepened with the passage of the years; a violin maker whose hands still reflect skills that have been honed to perfection from years of practice.

Not long ago as I was leaving a dinner party, I stopped to say good-bye to a man I have known most of my life. He is now in his late eighties, although he looks much younger. He was telling me about some artistic projects he wanted to finish, when his wife came over and added, "John needs to hire someone to do the yard work so that he can devote more time to his art. There are so many things he wants to do."

Too many things to do and not enough time to do them is not a state that fits our national stereotype of the elderly person who needs help in filling his or her days with relatively useless tasks. Former President Ronald Reagan, who in his late seventies fulfilled his duties with the vigor of a man much younger in years, did not fit the stereotype either. Yet the stereotype lives on, and old people and those of us who love them often feed into it.

Counseling the elderly is seen by some to be fairly nonproductive. "Old people don't change," they explain. In my experience as a family counselor, I have found that many elderly people change a great deal and some young people are already set in their ways. However, if counseling is to become a safety zone of change for the elderly, so that they can truly use these later years in their lives, it is vital that the young as well as the old believe that aging is not a curse but a blessing.

In *The Human Cycle*, Colin Turnbull describes certain African and Indian societies:

> The retirement expected of the aged does indeed
> also suppose that they retire from active participation
> in subsistence activities. But this is generally seen to
> be partly because they are no longer physically fitted
> to fill that economic role, or because there are others
> better fitted for that work, but more importantly be-
> cause there are other things that need to be done and
> which only the old can do. . . . They are relieved of
> one set of responsibilities so that they can fulfill an-
> other, equally vital role.[4]

Especially with the work potential extending into and
through the third quarter of life, many people grow elderly more slowly. They can be a part of the main work
force of this society for a much longer time. It is important,
however, that this "extra" period of productivity be used
because it is desired rather than frantically grabbed at as a
reprieve against what is seen as the inevitable curse of
retirement and old age. The third quarter should not be
used to hide from the aging process. When the years catch
up and some kind of retirement is necessary, there are
tasks to be done for which *only* the elderly are suited. The
tasks of old age are unique.

In my family some of us used to joke about my Aunt
Lydia being the historian of the family. She was. In her
late eighties she could still remember birthdays for those
of us who never could remember anyone else's. She could
recite long pieces of poetry in a way that reminded those
of us who were too caught up in the *doing* of life of the
value of refurbishing the spirit. She saved wedding an-
nouncements, pictures, newspaper clippings, wills, letters, bills of sale, and numerous other memorabilia from

more than a hundred years ago. She could identify a picture of someone like Aunt Sophie in Sweden, whom I had
never even heard about. Aunt Lydia not only performed a
service by her memory of family history and her practice
of collecting documents, but also in so doing cultivated a
sense of the continuity of life in younger family members.
We learned about the past from her. Most important, we
learned about *our* past from someone who had been an
active part of that past. Her task was unique.

As I was growing up, we lived next door to a German
family who became very close to us. When I was in those
early formative years, I remember thinking that these
neighbor children were so lucky because their grandparents came to live with them. The grandparents baby-
sat their grandchildren in a way that few paid persons
ever would. After all, they were their grandchildren.
Moreover, while the children were being taken care of
physically, they learned about their past.

Our family benefited, too. Sometimes we heard their
stories about the "olden times," or we tasted the venison
the grandfather smoked periodically in the outside "garden house." Recipes from the grandmother were enjoyed and then handed down, and fortunately for me
they were passed across the fence to my mother and ultimately to me.

Some of these recipes have become comfort food, reminding me of good times in the past and again fostering
in me that sense of the continuity of life. The old German
pancake recipe, for example, brings back childhood memories of spending the night next door, of sleeping in the
backyard and then sneaking back in because we were
afraid, and of eating our breakfast of pancakes served with

homemade syrup and freshly squeezed juice made from tangerines growing in our neighbors' backyard.

These recollections are a whole set of memories that are different from those associated with my mother's Swedish pancakes, which were made thin like crepes and then rolled up with syrup or strawberry jam. My mother's pancakes were a reminder of special times, sometimes served for company, at times made on rainy or gloomy days, or frequently served as Sunday night supper. Always they were accompanied by an ample supply of bacon. They, too, were comfort food, and both recipes continue to be comfort food in the present for both families, recipes handed down from those who have gone on before.

Regardless of the meaningfulness of tasks uniquely suited to those who are elderly, there is no reason why, as we age, we should retire from our regular work before we need to or must. We don't have to go from the extreme of avoiding the aging process to the other extreme of prematurely embracing it. Moreover, when we have retired, there is nothing wrong with enjoying life, taking trips abroad, cultivating a hobby, and enjoying the comradeship of other elderly people. To fill up retirement time with shuffleboard and bingo, just because there's nothing else to do, however, is to waste a very valuable period of life. We as a nation and as individuals often waste the vast resources of old age.

An older lady who recently found herself alone and without family was advised by many to go to a senior center for recreation. Later she told me, "I know that places like these meet the needs of many, but not mine. I've decided to work with children who can't read. I have the time, and that's partly what they need." For her, helping children develop a love for the written word has been a fulfilling task, and it has utilized a valuable resource in the community. Teaching children was a rewarding task *for her;* it would not be for others. The unique function of the last years of life should be considered as carefully and prepared for as completely as that of any other time of life. These times are not throwaway years any more than any other period of life.

Although I do not advocate lengthening the dying process beyond its time or approve of ridiculous attempts to keep a body "alive" long after it was meant to be let go, I do believe in living life to its full length and in valuing life at every stage. I am deeply concerned when the years of old age are looked on as throwaway years, at best to be enjoyed in a limited way with amusements designed to satisfy the superficial whims of a second childhood. Such an attitude is contrary to the biblical concept that age is a reward, a time of honor, and a time of instructing those who are younger.

In his New Testament letter to Titus, Paul commands Titus:

> Teach the older men to be serious and unruffled; they must be sensible, knowing and believing the truth and doing everything with love and patience. Teach the older women to be quiet and respectful . . . they should be teachers of goodness. These older women must train the younger women. . . .
>
> (Titus 2:2–4 TLB)

These, too, are part of the works of old age. It is the province of the church to teach such a view of old age to

its members. In that way, children will take such an attitude for granted as they grow up. Caretakers of the elderly
will treat them with respect, with the result that the elderly will take themselves seriously and act with greater
dignity. Again, we tend to become what people expect us
to become.

Activities for the elderly are not just amusements to
placate their restlessness or to keep them from bothering
anyone. The seriousness of these tasks restores the dignity
of age to a society that has at times so drastically lost that
sense of dignity that it must go to the Third World for
examples of the value of old age, a value based on its
proximity to death and its reservoir of knowledge from the
past.

In speaking of those who retire and are through with
the physically productive period of their lives, Colin Turnbull concludes:

> Those who dream only of all the things they are
> going to "do" fail to find the state of grace in just
> being. And the more they try to do, the more they
> find that they cannot do; the longer and harder they
> try, the more the recognition of their ultimate failure
> is impressed upon them. Their golf handicap in-
> creases; they win fewer and fewer games of chess;
> their fingers are less nimble on the keyboard; increas-
> ingly they forget to water their prize-winning flowers;
> their eyesight fails them and makes it difficult and
> painful to read those unread books. They compete
> with themselves as well as with others and with life
> itself to the bitter end. . . .
>
> The more an adult is convinced of his worth at
> retirement, the harder it is for him to navigate the

transition into an old age which we have made into a world of doing nothing. Its patent emptiness and irrelevance to anyone but their isolated selves often leads to rapid physical or mental deterioration and premature death, or even to suicide. The stereotyped suicide notes that say, "Nobody wants me" and "I am of no use to anyone anymore" are not necessarily penned by individuals in a moment of self-pity; they may well be simple, sober assessments of an agonizing and protracted reality to which, for a socially conscious human being in our individualistic society, only one answer may seem logical.[5]

If we live long enough, we grow old. The only way to avoid old age is to die young. If we are old long enough, our active productivity will diminish. Our bodies and even our minds may slow down. It is then that we can *be*. We can worship God from a different vantage point than ever before. More than ever, we can praise Him for all that He has done, but we can also worship Him for all that He is. We can offer up the work of prayer for others with insight that is forbidden to the very young. Furthermore, in old age more than at any other time, we can provide a connection with the past for those who are younger. It is then that we can be a vital link in the continuity of life.

My friend Joseph Fabry escaped from Austria and eventually Europe during the time of Hitler's takeover. In his book, cowritten with a lifelong friend, Dr. Fabry describes his discouragement when, after reaching America, he realized the dismal prospects for getting his parents out of Europe. In the letters he received from home, he learned that friends and relatives had gradually disappeared, and my friend realized with increasing clarity that his roots were being ripped away from him. He had experienced a violent disruption in the continuity of life.

In *One and One Make Three*, Dr. Fabry explains:

> As so often happened, one significant incident provided a hint of an answer. I chatted with a woman who helped Horch translate his German authors. She was a seventh-generation American, her ancestor having come two hundred years ago. I said, I wished I had an ancestor like that, and she replied: "Why, *you* are an ancestor." This chance remark shifted my attention from shortcomings in the past to potentials in the future. I lost my family in Europe but could start my own in America! . . . a search had begun for a new relatedness.[6]

He had started the beginning of a new thread of the continuity of life, a thread he is now passing on to his children and their children.

We all need that sense of the continuity of our own individual lives on this earth. We need to be part of a past that is bigger than any one person. The elderly provide this for us, sometimes just in our memories of them long after they have left this earth. Not long ago on a St. Patrick's Day I was in my office, listening to a patient, when I heard an old Irish melody playing on the radio in the next room. My Swedish father was very fond of Irish tunes and would often sing or whistle one. The song on the radio had been one of his favorites. For a moment I felt a warm closeness to my father, who died a number of years ago. Happy memories flooded back, and I went on through the day with a sense of happy security that connected my past with my present and my future. Partly because of my father, my life was part of a whole; it had continuity.

When I was twelve, my mother and I went back to our old home in Chicago for the summer. It was a time of sight-seeing and visiting relatives. On a hot Sunday afternoon, my mother and I went to Great-aunt Christine's house for a small family reunion. I was the only child present that I remember, and at first I felt a little left out. The house was a lovely old structure, well kept up and impeccably furnished. All the chairs had white lace doilies on their backs and the tables had ruffled doilies under the lamps and vases. Everything was starched, and clean, and perfect. In the middle of it all was Great-aunt Christine, with her white hair softly rolled up on top of her head with a perfection that equalled that of the house. Everyone sat drinking coffee from finely decorated china cups, and the conversation flowed around me.

"Would you like a glass of cold grape juice?" someone behind me asked. It was my Great-aunt Christine's son, Warner Sallman, who had painted the well-loved head of Christ. He was probably the only famous person there, but to a child he was more impressive for his kindness than for his paintings. I don't remember what else he or anyone else said after that, but I do remember that I suddenly felt part of this large group of people of varying ages. Even though I didn't know most of them, they were my family. Someday I would be adult like them and drink coffee from china cups instead of grape juice from a glass. Someday I would be respected and honored like Great-aunt Christine. I was part of a whole, and for the moment at the center of that wholeness was an elderly lady whom I would never really know personally but whom I would never forget. On that hot afternoon so long ago, all that was needed was for her just to be. That was the unique function of her old age.

As the race of life slows down for the elderly, others, themselves at varying stages of aging, watch anxiously by the sidelines. For them the aging of those they love is a signpost of what is ahead. They are reminded that they, too, will sometime age and die. They may try to deny the realities of old age by cheering the elderly on to almost lethal doses of activity or they may begin to ignore their elderly friends and relatives, or prematurely put them into so-called retirement homes, where they'll be "with their own kind," as though they were some new breed of human being. They make excuses not to visit. They pretend that the elderly are not there. They deny their existence and then use the fast deterioration of the elderly as further proof of the curse of old age, rather than realizing that the deterioration has been, in part, a result of their own attitude of discouragement.

If watching the elderly grow older is a signpost to the young of what is ahead, the actual death of a parent is a blinking red light of one's own mortality. The day before my mother's funeral was a very trying day for me. I had expected to feel down, but I had not expected to feel a sort of nagging anxiety as though something I could not completely identify was wrong. I read my Bible; I took a hot bubble bath; I talked to some friends; I went out to dinner. I did all the things I usually do to relax, and none of them helped.

Then I picked up a copy of Madeleine L'Engle's *The Summer of the Great Grandmother*. Toward the end of the book the author makes the comment, "I will never again be anyone's child." In that one statement I recognized my own feelings. That was the anxiety. In my mother's death I had passed another signpost. She was the second parent to die. The last. I was now truly adult. I was now the authority rather than the one who still, once in a while, looked to my mother's authority. I had been an adult for a long time. But now there was no turning back. Moreover, not only was I now completely adult, but also I had moved up a notch in that inevitable journey toward my own death.

With the recognition of my own feelings in that simple line, "I will never again be anyone's child," a great peace settled upon me. I knew what was wrong, and it was not "wrong" at all. I had seen the signpost: "You are now *the* adult; you will never again be anyone's child." The signpost had frightened me at first. Then, when I understood what the signpost was truly saying, I felt that I had been promoted to a new position of responsibility and challenge. I felt that God was now calling me to provide to those around me the support and help that I had received from my mother and from others like her. The next day I went to my mother's funeral with grief but also with hope for the future.

Seventeenth-century poet John Donne's idea that no man is an island and that every man's death diminishes each of us is true in connection with our view of the elderly in a different sense, perhaps, than that meant by Donne. Their death diminishes us because we fear that we are next. We make feeble attempts to ignore the elderly, as if by denying their existence we can reaffirm the myth that we ourselves will never age, or at least not in the near future!

At the same time we are busy denying the aging process in others, in our own lives we gloomily prepare for our own aging with over-the-hill jokes about that milestone birthday *fifty*. We are filled with regret rather than the reward of the years. Anti-aging creams and cosmetic surgery postpone the ravages of time for yet a while. All this because, above all, we ourselves fear the specter of age and ultimately death.

The Judeo-Christian tradition has always included a belief in the hereafter. Yet to many of us old age still marks the End and thus becomes something to avoid.

In contrast, other cultures that believe in an afterlife view the proximity of the aged to death or eternity as something very positive. They are revered because they become a link to the spirit world. Anthropologist Colin Turnbull says:

> Certainly in other cultures, particularly those with a firm belief in an after or other life, the old are accorded a position of often enormous respect and honor. . . . They are ignored, in our society, for the very thing that makes them so immensely powerful in other societies: their proximity to death. That is, perhaps, what we need most to explore, this association in other cultures of the old with that vast source of power, Spirit power, that lies beyond death. It provides a whole new perspective on old age.[7]

Lest this sound too mystical to us, let us remember that we Christians, too, have our own perspective on "Spirit power" that can be of great help and comfort to us. In spite of the fact that our culture has abused the reality of and blurred the meaning of a term like *Spirit power* by our society's focus on demonic or even so-called neutral supernatural forces, Heaven and God Almighty still exist. We still deal with a supernatural God with supernatural powers that far outdo anything Satan can attempt to imitate. Indeed, such imitation on the part of Satan is to be expected, for if there is no reality, there is no counterfeit.

Long before Turnbull used the term, and long before the concept became perverted into occult connotations, men and women of God have evidenced a sense of Spirit power in their treatment of old age and death. Within us is an innate need for a God Connection. Old Testament saints did not avoid deathbed scenes: a deathbed was often a place where the dying person—this person who was now so close to Heaven—spoke wise words to those who remained.

When King David was about to die, he spoke to his son Solomon:

> I am going where every man on earth must some day go. I am counting on you to be a strong and worthy successor. Obey the laws of God and follow all his ways; keep each of his commands written in the law of Moses so that you will prosper in everything you do, wherever you turn. If you do this, then the Lord will fulfill the promise he gave me, that if my children and their descendants watch their step and are faithful to God, one of them shall always be the king of Israel—my dynasty will never end.
>
> (1 Kings 2:2–4 LL)

Consistent with the deathbed exhortation of King David, the Old Testament deathbed was often the scene of the conferring of a blessing. In Genesis 27:4 Isaac is old and is anticipating his death when he asks Esau to "make me savoury meat . . . that I may eat; that my soul may bless thee before I die." In their commentary Jamieson, Faisset, and Brown note:

> The deathbed benediction of the patriarchs was not simply the last farewell blessing of a father to his children, though that, pronounced with all the fulness and energy of concentrated feeling, carries in every word an impressive significance which penetrates the inmost parts of the filial heart, and is often felt there long after the tongue that uttered it is silent in the grave. The dying benediction of the patriarchs had a mysterious import; it was a supernatural act. . . . It was, in fact, a testamentary conveyance of the promise, bequeathed with great solemnity in a formal address, called a *blessing;* which, consisting partly of prayers and partly of predictions, was an authoritative appropriation of the covenant promises to the person who inherited the right of primogeniture.[8]

This God Connection is more clearly understandable to the Christian in the familiar yet often ignored words of Hebrews 12:1: "Wherefore seeing we also are compassed about with so great a cloud of witnesses, let us lay aside every weight, and the sin which doth so easily beset us, and let us run with patience the race that is set before us." Those who have gone before are still linked with us. They cheer us on. Those who are closer by age to death than we are, but who are still with us, are becoming a link with us to eternity.

I experienced something of the truth of Hebrews 12:1 after my mother's death, when I wrote in my personal journal:

> I am alone. I will never again be anyone's child. But I can go on and live in my friendships and do and become those things which were meant for my life— my writing, my therapy—and above all honor God. In these ways I will deserve my parents' trust in me. I love them both and will always miss them. But I must go on, for "I have miles to go before I sleep."

Most of my relatives were in Heaven when I wrote those words, but I still felt the comfort of my family's approval; I was motivated by my belief that they were now, perhaps more than ever before, cheering me on. On earth they saw in part, but now they have seen our Lord face-to-face, and they see the whole.

In Old Testament history, while Israel was still in the wilderness after leaving Egypt, God told Moses to send spies into Canaan to "search the land" (Num. 13:2). They were to bring back a report on the unknown to those who were still safely behind its borders. Some told of giants in the land; others spoke of a land that flowed with milk and honey.

Part of the special God Connection of those who grow old and approach Heaven is that they tell us what they see as they approach the Land. They make a report. To some there are giants in the transition between life and death. There can be a fear of the process of dying, even when people know Christ and are therefore sure of their eternal destiny after death. Dying is not always just falling asleep.

Sometimes it involves pain and struggle. For until we are actually with God, we still cope with the frailty of this human body of ours. But for the Christian who looks beyond the human discomfort, the Land itself "floweth with milk and honey" (Num. 13:27).

A number of years ago as my father lay on a hospital bed close to death, he was asked how things were with him. He replied succinctly, "It is the grace of God which has brought me thus far, and it is that grace of God which will bring me through." He gave a good report of that Land to which He was going.

I remembered years before when as a child I used to hear him stand up in the mid-week prayer meeting and recite the Twenty-third Psalm: ". . . though I walk through the valley of the shadow of death, I will fear no evil: for thou art with me. . . ." Now, close to the time of his departure to be with his Lord, the report was still good. His words encouraged me more than anything else at that time. It became his gift to me as he died. It was his truest legacy to his children. The Land to which he was going was okay; we didn't need to fear aging and death.

Although the process of dying is not something that most of us look forward to, for those who have placed their faith in Christ physical death itself means to be in the presence of our Lord. Unless we choose to end our lives ourselves, that precise moment in our history when we are ushered into His presence has been determined by God from before the foundation of the earth. The timing of each of our deaths is no mistake. Death is not limited to the aged. But whatever our life span, we do not need to fear that we will not finish the course that God has set for us. Our living and our dying are in His time.

To those who are not old but fear what will happen to them when they are old, Charles Spurgeon has some very comforting words:

> Now, you middle-aged men, you are plunged into the midst of business, and are sometimes supposing what will become of you in your old age. . . . You say, "Suppose I should live to be as old as So-and-so, and be a burden upon the people, I should not like that." Don't get meddling with God's business; leave his decrees to him. There is many a person who thought he would die in a workhouse that has died in a mansion; and many a woman that has thought she would die in the streets, has died in her bed, happy and comfortable. . . . Middle-aged man! listen to what David says again, "I have been young, and now am old; yet I have not seen the righteous forsaken, nor his seed begging bread." Go on, then . . . leave thy declining years to him, and give thy present years to him.[9]

In a society that attempts to deny death, even when we are in its very presence, by trying to make the dead look "natural" in their coffins, it is perhaps to be expected that we should deny death before it occurs by hiding the elderly and pretending that we ourselves are not so close to death after all. Yet, more often than not, in confronting such fears rather than denying them we see them in their true perspective.

To provide a place for such confrontation has traditionally been the province of the church. Yet increasingly I have people come into the safety zone of my counseling office in order to sort out and discuss without fear of censure their views, doubts, and fears regarding death and what comes after death.

In the 1951 movie version of Stephen Crane's *Red Badge of Courage*, a young man fighting in the Civil War fears death in battle and fears fear itself. After the agony of experiencing the cowardice of running from battle and the exhilaration of great courage as he carries the flag into the greatest heat of battle, he goes home in triumph over his fear. At the end the narrator says, "As he trudged from the place of blood and wrath his soul changed. He had been to touch the Great Death and found that, after all, it was but the Great Death."

In the same way we, too, deal with our own mortality as we deal with the aged. In childhood and youth we feel immortal. The young are reckless because they do not yet appreciate the frailty of life. As we view those around us growing old, and even the young sometimes dying, we begin to view our own mortality. Our relationship with the aged can provide a graceful transition between youth and age for us which, if we miss it, just makes our own aging that much more difficult. Ultimately, as we view others' transition into old age, we find that, as well as being mortal on this earth, we are truly immortal souls.

CHAPTER EIGHT

MAKING BAD TIMES GOOD

For months Neil had been sleeping with various women he met on business trips. His wife, Margarita, had never found out about any of the affairs, but she had noticed an emotional wall rising between them. Then suddenly one Monday afternoon Neil called home to tell Margarita that he was leaving her for good. "You're fat and ugly!" he exclaimed with cruelty. "I want someone younger."

The truth was that Margarita had remained slim and attractive but Neil had put on thirty pounds during the preceding year. That fact, added to his celebration of his fortieth birthday, a milestone he commemorated by spending the day getting drunk, was probably the real motivator in spurring Neil to find out how attractive he could still be to women.

Margarita was left with four children: two teenage sons and two children of grammar-school age. Neil's support checks were sporadic. Because Margarita had never worked outside her home, she was panicky at first. Then someone advised her, "Just think about what you do best and do it."

Margarita had developed into a wonderful cook over the past two decades. A friend had been having trouble making a success of a small snack bar, even though it was well located near some construction sites. The friend made a gentleman's agreement with Margarita that if she could make the snack bar at least break even, he would give her a partnership in the business and share the proceeds with her.

Full of excitement, Margarita went to work. She decided that the snack bar drew little interest because the food was not only routine and dull but also poorly prepared. An expert in soups, Margarita started making her own home-made specialties, a different soup every day. She served the soup with freshly baked corn bread. Her cooking was a success. People not only flocked there for lunch, but also called ahead to reserve bowls of soup. Within six months the snack bar was a real money-maker.

Then one morning the owner came in to visit. "I appreciate all you've done," he commented, after obtaining copies of her recipes. "This is great soup." Then he explained that he was going to let his son take over the business; he wouldn't need her anymore. There was no contract. After all, they had been friends, and she had trusted him.

As Margarita told me her story two years later, it made *me* angry, even if she did seem to be handling it. "That's okay," she said reassuringly. "I got something from it. I learned that everyone liked my homemade soup and corn bread. I was okay, after all."

As a counselor I have discovered that a determining factor in how much difficulty we have with handling hard times is whether we view our cup as half empty or half full. In a sense Margarita had lost it all: her husband, her source of income, and even her faith in a friend. However, she saw that her cup was half full. She had proven to herself that Neil's problems were his own. She was okay. With her confidence restored, she has been paid in currency more precious than gold.

During recent years, it seems to me, we have had an inordinate number of natural disasters across this country. Floods, hurricanes, earthquakes, tornados, and fires have filled the nightly news reports. Through the rather bizarre way reporters have of interviewing people just as disaster has devastated their lives, we sometimes gain remarkable insight into people's immediate reactions to personal loss and bad times.

After a disaster, two general groups of people seem to emerge. One says, understandably, "Everything is gone. I don't know what to do. We've lost everything we've worked for." Another says, pointing to the ashes on the ground, "That's what's left, and the insurance will only cover a small amount of the losses. Photographs and personal belongings can't be replaced. But we're so lucky. No one died. We still have each other."

Many in the first group eventually move over to the second, once the initial shock is past, and a few from the second group may fall back into the first. But how well anyone who experiences bad times can make them into good times will hinge on whether the person focuses on the cup as half full or half empty.

Not long ago, after working all evening on paying my

bills, I was surprised to find that I was able to pay more bills at one time than I had first anticipated. I went to bed happy over that fact. I still had bills to be paid, but those obligations would be met and my focus was on what I had been able to pay already. My cup was half full.

The next morning I woke up with a jolt. My focus had changed: I still had unpaid bills. All the relief of the previous evening was gone. The night before I had said to myself, "My bills are in pretty good shape." Now, the next morning, I was asking, "What if I can't pay my bills on time?" My cup had become half empty.

After an operation for cancer, someone once said to me, "I'm lucky. Most people live from day to day in a sort of unconscious manner. They assume their days are unlimited. Then suddenly life is over, and they've never really done what they wanted with those days. I've had a red blinking light go off. I *know* my days are limited. I will use those days better now than I would have if I had never had cancer."

When this person related these feelings to her physician, he just shook his head and said, "You have an amazing attitude." In reality, it was a sound attitude. It was looking at a cup as half full rather than half empty. It reminded me of a story I once read of two men in a prison who looked out their prison window. One saw mud, and one saw blue sky.

In the little gray book into which I used to copy quotations from the blackboard during my high school senior English class, one quotation, written by an unknown source, adds an apt insight to the half-empty, half-full image:

The optimist fell ten stories.
At each window bar
He shouted to his friends:
"All right so far."

Trite? Perhaps. Homey? Definitely. Nevertheless, in these whimsical lines there is truth that has existed throughout human history. Life *is* deadly serious. Yet, in spite of that seriousness—and perhaps because of it—we dare not embark upon the challenge of living without a sense of humor and the ability to see through the rain to the rainbow.

Hard times are indeed far from trite. As Ruth Bell Graham said in my interview with her: "It's so easy to be superficial or to speak too quickly." Mrs. Graham went on, "There are some things that come crushing down on lives that are far too heavy to lift." For those things there is the biblical injunction to commit our way unto the Lord. The Hebrew word for *commit*, explained Mrs. Graham, means "to roll." "We can roll something that is so great a weight that we cannot possibly lift it. . . . It takes years of learning that He never lets us down. . . . It doesn't mean that He doesn't disappoint us. . . . He doesn't always give in to us. . . . He doesn't always answer our prayers the way we want Him to. But so much the better in the long run."

During the major times of crisis in our lives, the pain may be excruciating at first. An admonition to make lemons into lemonade will only be an insult. Lemonade may come much later, after the raw wounds have healed. Mrs. Graham's image for those times that are particularly difficult is that of an *abscess*, which according to the dictionary is "a localized collection of pus surrounded by inflamed tissue." Said Mrs. Graham, "You have to let time for an abscess to come to head before you can lance it. . . . When you once lance it and the pus is drained off, then the healing can begin. It's a slow process, but it's an important process."

Sometimes the counseling office is the place where abscesses are lanced, and the bitterness, fear, and anger are vented in safety. It is important that enough time is given for this initial process; however, focus must be turned as soon as possible to going on. The cup must once again be viewed as half full. The time must come, too, for making lemonade. For although we cannot always choose the circumstances of our lives, we can choose our attitude toward those circumstances.

Not long ago *Time* magazine carried an article by Richard Behar entitled "Warlocks, Witches and Swastikas." It told of vandalism by four young people against a prominent rabbi, as well as against other Jews. Some wanted the boys exposed by having their names printed in the newspaper; others wanted revenge. In contrast, the rabbi wanted to be part of the healing.

A year prior to the incident, the rabbi had lost his son. A few months after the attack, the rabbi had heart surgery. Yet after the court hearing, he started teaching twenty-five hours of Jewish culture to four boys who had assaulted his home but whom he now invited into his temple. The rabbi had chosen his attitude toward his given set of circumstances. He had focused on healing four boys who had harmed him, rather than focusing on his pain.

Mark was only five when his mother died and his father abandoned him in a car parked in a vacant lot. The police found him, and he was placed in a foster home with a kindly older couple. For the next year, Mark lived with nightmares of being abandoned. At school the older children teased him about belonging to the state. He became spiteful and vengeful, which only got him into trouble with his teacher. Regular visits from his social worker and occasional interviews by couples who "wanted to take him out and be his 'special friends' " were constant reminders that his placement was temporary and that adoption by some stranger was imminent.

More devastating than anything else, in his mind's eye he kept seeing his father walking away from him in the parking lot, while Mark screamed, "Daddy, Daddy, don't leave me here alone." His father had kept walking until he had disappeared around the corner.

Then one Sunday morning Mark went to Sunday school and learned about Christ. He learned also that Heaven was a place where we would see those we had loved on earth. In his prayers that night, Mark prayed:

Dear God,
Please come and live in my life. And please
make my Daddy love you too. Then we can at
least live together in heaven.

From that time on, Mark was a much happier little boy. Nothing in his outward circumstances had really changed: his father was still missing, couples still made him their "special friend," and the children at school still teased him. However, Mark had found a heavenly Father who cared about him and who wouldn't abandon him in a parking lot. He had hope, too, of seeing his earthly father again, at least in Heaven. Even at his early age, Mark had changed from seeing a half-empty cup to one that was half full. He had turned his bad times into good.

Choosing our attitude toward a given set of circumstances is easier, and sometimes only possible, if we look away from the circumstances that surround us to focus on God. Missionary Amy Carmichael was fond of saying, "All that troubles is only for a moment. Nothing is important but that which is eternal."[1] This concept has often held me from resentment and despair as I have realized that God never wastes suffering. Everything that happens to us is allowed or sent by God and has eternal purpose, regardless of whether we understand it all now.

As I was falling asleep the other night, my mind drifted to the theme of making bad times good. It occurred to me that God always carefully measures out our suffering. In contrast, His blessings are poured out upon us freely and without measure. Furthermore, how much we turn unavoidable suffering into blessing by choosing our attitude toward that suffering will be a determining factor in the state of our mental health.

In a striking illustration of how much God may be doing in our lives that we can't understand or see, Charles Spurgeon once preached about a woman who went to a place where they were manufacturing a carpet. As she looked at the carpet which was being made, she said, "There is no beauty there."

The owner objected, "It is one of the most beautiful carpets you ever saw."

Still committed to the idea that the carpet was ugly, the woman criticized, "Why here is a piece hanging out, and it is all in disorder."

"Do you know why, ma'am?" the man said once again, in disagreement. Then, in answer to his own question, he said, "You look at the wrong side."[2]

A friend of mine called recently with a tone of excitement in his voice. "Do you remember the illustration about the carpet, and seeing the wrong side?" he asked. "Well, I just came back from a trip. I went to a factory where they make lovely wall hangings and carpets. It really is just like we heard. Underneath, as you stand on the floor and look up at the loom, the carpet looks terrible. There is no design, and all kinds of different colored loose ends hang down. But then, when someone takes the loom down and shows you the right side, the pattern is beautiful."

Sometimes on this earth we see only the underneath side of what God is making out of our lives. We see the frayed ends and what looks like a meaningless pattern of events. God sees it all from a divine perspective. He sees the beautiful, finished product of our lives. At times He gives us a glimpse of what we are becoming, and we are encouraged. Then, when we focus on the eternal purposes of our lives, our cup once again becomes half full, not half empty.

The safety zone of counseling is a place where people can discover how to make bad times good. For the Christian it can also be a place of discovering the talents God has given us and more about the tapestry God is weaving into our lives.

A colleague of mine once said, "Life is a little like the ocean. The tide always goes out and it always comes in. When the tide is out, it looks as though it will always stay out. When it is in, it looks as though it will never go back out. But the tide always comes in, and it always goes out. It does not remain constant."

Bad and good times both are the lot of all men and women. This is life. Unlike the tide, however, we each have a choice: we can focus on the retreating tide, which seems to be taking all of our dreams out with it, or we can focus on the fact that the tide truly does come back in with all its fullness. Life changes, for good and for bad, but what we do with what life provides us can make all the difference between making it and not making it in this world. Unlike the inanimate piece of tapestry my friend watched being woven, we humans have a choice in co-operating with what God is making of our lives.

Not long ago a college professor who had been seeing me about work-related issues as well as some self-esteem problems came for his last appointment. When Bill first started his counseling sessions, he was intimidated by what he viewed as his colleagues' superior backgrounds in teaching. Furthermore, his students frightened him, and so his relationship with them was stilted and formal. Like so many people with low self-esteem, Bill focused on himself and on what people thought of him.

As he gained self-esteem and developed skills in declaring and in time management, Bill became an effective teacher. He learned to say no to unreasonable demands, and he planned his work so that he had time for more social activities. Understandably, his stress level was greatly reduced.

At his final meeting with me, Bill slumped down into the familiar leather chair, put his feet up on the footstool, and said with a grin, "With all the changes in curriculum this year, I wouldn't have begun to make it a year ago.

Now the newness just seems like an enjoyable challenge." What would once have been a nightmare of defeat had become a platform for growth; what other teachers were viewing as a bad year for teaching had become a good year for Bill.

Recycling is a popular concept in our world as we draw near the end of the twentieth century and enter the twenty-first century. Paper products and tin cans that have served their purpose are now made usable again in this time of too much throwaway waste, too little space, and seemingly too many people. Recycling is becoming a necessity for survival.

In the emotional and spiritual realm, recycling is also a necessity for survival. In the safety zone of counseling, people learn to take lives with shattered dreams and rebuild them into something very new and wonderful. Instead of being destroyed by the past, they build in the present; instead of living with regrets over the past, they live in hopes of the future.

In the movie *Shadowlands,* which portrays the latter part of the life of C. S. Lewis, a colleague says to Lewis, "I don't have your faith in divine recycling." For the Christian the recycling process is more than a humanistic attempt to make people better. The Christian God is the Great Recycler, and sometimes He uses the counselor and the place of counseling as tools in His divine recycling.

In speaking of the physical body, Lewis once wrote in a letter:

> Like old automobiles, aren't they? where all sorts
> of apparently different things keep going wrong, but
> what they add up to is the plain fact that the machine

is wearing out. Well, it was not meant to last forever. Still, I have a kindly feeling for the old rattle-trap. Through it God showed me that whole side of His beauty which is embodied in colour, sound, smell and size.[3]

The same ideas could be expressed regarding the human mind. Who could be better at recycling either the mind or the body, the emotions or the spirit, than the One who designed them and created them to start with?

Ultimately, therefore, when we speak of counseling and change, we must concur with the well-known psychotherapist Rollo May, who says:

Finally, after all our discussion, we come to the realization that there is a great area in the transformation of personality which we do not understand, and which we can attribute only to the mysterious creativity of life. . . . As the motto has it, "The physician furnishes the conditions—God works the cure." Like the doctor, we may bind up the wound, but there are all the forces of life welling up in their incalculable spontaneity in the growing together of skin and nerve tissues and the reflowing of blood to perform the healing. Before the creative forces of life, the true counselor stands humbly. And his humility is not of the false sort, for the deeper his understanding of personality the more clearly he realizes how minute his efforts in comparison to the greatness of the whole. He says with the psalmist, "Lord, that is too wonderful for me." I am myself frank to say that when the limits of my own understanding are reached. I understand the miracle of transformation of personality in terms of the age-old but ever new concept, the grace of God.[4]

After my mother's death there followed a three-year process of working through things, papers, business details, and family problems. Everyone in my family had been dying, seemingly at once, and so I was faced with details involving the deaths of several people, all of whom were very dear to me. Memories were constant, as was my fatigue. Although there were some wonderful times of respite, encouragement, and even happiness, for much of the time, my cup had seemed half empty.

On a Friday afternoon shortly before Thanksgiving, after I finished some details that marked, symbolically, the end of the deaths and the beginning of normal life, a friend and I drove up a street toward my apartment. It was a rainy day, the kind where it always looks as if the rain is going to stop but it doesn't. Normally I love rain, but on this particular day the slow drizzle matched my mood: nothing extreme, just flat.

Then I looked up into the rain-filled sky and saw a rainbow. The tightness I had felt inside relaxed. Through blinding tears I watched those soft colors of hope until they finally disappeared into the sky once again, and then I was left with a deep sense of worship and gratitude toward God. My cup had seemed so empty, and now it suddenly seemed so full once again. Culminating in that brief moment, my life had been divinely recycled. Bad times had once again become good.

ENDNOTES

Chapter One: Dream Blockers

1. Winston S. Churchill, *Painting as a Pastime* (New York: Cornerstone Library, 1965), 7–8.
2. Churchill *Painting* 16.
3. Churchill *Painting* 31.
4. Margaret Millar, *Wall of Eyes* (reprint, New York: International Polygonics, Ltd., 1986), 176.
5. Anton Gill, *The Journey Back from Hell* (New York: William Morrow & Co., Inc., 1988), 456.
6. Peter Fabrizius (Max Knight and Joseph Fabry), *One and One Make Three* (Berkeley, Calif.: Benmir Books, 1988), 3–4.
7. Richard Nixon, *In the Arena* (New York: Simon & Schuster, 1990), 157–58.

Chapter Two: Dream Bashers

1. George Matheson, "Make Me a Captive, Lord," originally called "Christian Freedom" in *Sacred Songs* (Row Dumbartonshire, Scotland, 1890). Source Robert Guy McCutcheon, *Our Hymnody: A Manual of the Methodist Hymnal,* with an index of scriptural texts, 2nd edition (New York: Abingdon Cokesbury Press, 1937), 384.
2. C. S. Lewis, *Mere Christianity* (New York: Macmillan, 1964), 162.

Chapter Three: Playing Cheetah

1. Winston S. Churchill, *Painting as a Pastime* (New York: Cornerstone Library, 1965), 7.
2. Churchill *Painting* 9-10.
3. Charles H. Spurgeon, source unknown.

Chapter Four: A Safety Zone of Discovery

1. Paul Tournier et al., *A Place for You* (New York: Harper & Row, 1968), 79.
2. Rollo May, *The Art of Counseling* (Nashville: Abingdon, 1967), 119.
3. Tournier *Place* 22.
4. Anton Gill, *The Journey Back from Hell* (New York: William Morrow, 1988), 328.
5. Martin Niemöller, *Dachau Sermons,* trans. Robert H. Pfeiffer (New York and London: Harper & Brothers, 1946), 78–79.
6. Miep Gies with Alison Leslie Gold, *Anne Frank Remembered* (New York: Simon & Schuster, 1987), 139.
7. C. S. Lewis et al., *The Inklings* (Boston: Houghton Mifflin Company, 1979), 45.
8. Sigmund Freud, quoted in M. D. Sackler et al., "Recent Advances in Psychobiology and Their Impact on General Practice," *Inter. Record of Med.* 170 (1957): 1551.

9. Henry Hyde, *For Every Idle Silence* (Ann Arbor: Servant Books, 1985), 108.

Chapter Five: Dream Blocks

1. Kenneth S. Wuest, *Romans in the Greek New Testament* (Grand Rapids: William B. Eerdmans Publishing Co., 1955), 209–11.
2. C. S. Lewis, *The Weight of Glory* (Grand Rapids: William B. Eerdmans Publishing Co., 1965), 15.
3. Søren Kierkegaard, *A Kierkegaard Anthology*, ed. Robert Bretall (Princeton, N.J.: Princeton University Press, 1946), 289, as quoted in Rollo May, *Man's Search for Himself* (New York: W. W. Norton, 1953), 101.
4. Lewis *Weight* 40–41.
5. Lewis *Weight* 9.
6. Lewis *Weight* 8–9.
7. Rollo May, *Man's Search for Himself* (New York: W.W. Norton, 1953), 100.
8. Socrates, quoted in May *Man's Search* 99.
9. Adolf Hitler, *Mein Kampf*, as quoted in William L. Shirer, *The Rise and Fall of the Third Reich* (New York: Simon & Schuster, 1959), 26.
10. Goethe quoted in Viktor E. Frankl et al., *Are You Nobody?* (Richmond: John Knox Press, 1973), 30.
11. Paul Tournier, *The Meaning of Persons* (New York: Harper & Row, 1957), 50.
12. Edward J. Boyer, "Consummate Entertainer Sammy Davis Jr. Dies at 64," *Los Angeles Times*, 17 March 1990, p. A28.

Chapter Six: Dream Builders

1. Viktor E. Frankl, *The Doctor and the Soul* (New York: Vintage, Random House, 1973), ix, xv.
2. Paul Tournier et al., *A Place for You* (New York: Harper & Row, 1968), 78–79.
3. Amy Carmichael, *Thou Givest—They Gather* (Fort Washington, PA: Christian Literature Crusade) 70–71.
4. Viktor E. Frankl et al., *Are You Nobody?* (Richmond: John Knox Press, 1973), 58.
5. Frankl *Are You Nobody?* 58.
6. Frankl *Are You Nobody?* 19.
7. Walter Trobisch, *The Complete Works of Walter Trobisch* (Downers Grove, Ill.: Inter-Varsity Press, 1987), 661.
8. C. S. Lewis, *Mere Christianity* (New York: Macmillan, 1964), 80–82.
9. C. S. Lewis, *Letters to an American Lady* (Grand Rapids: William B. Eerdmans Publishing Co., 1967), 41.
10. G. K. Chesterton, *St. Francis of Assisi* (London: Hodder & Stoughton), 110, as quoted in Tournier, *The Meaning of Persons* (New York: Harper & Row, 1957), 183.

Chapter Seven: The God Connection

1. Charles H. Spurgeon, *Sermons of Rev. C. H. Spurgeon* (New York: Funk & Wagnalls, 1857), vol. 2, 366.
2. William Manchester, *American Caesar: Douglas MacArthur 1880–1964* (Boston: Little, Brown & Co., 1978), 702.
3. Alan Pifer and Lydia Bronte, eds., *Our Aging Society* (New York: W. W. Norton, 1986), 4, 11, 12.
4. Colin Turnbull, *The Human Cycle* (New York: Touchstone, Simon & Schuster, 1983), 229.
5. Turnbull *Human Cycle* 257–58.
6. Peter Fabrizius (with Max Knight and Joseph Fabry), *One*

and One Make Three (Berkeley, Calif.: Benmir Books, 1988), 131.

7. Turnbull *Human Cycle* 226.
8. Rev. Robert Jamieson, D.D., Rev. A. R. Fausset, A.M., Rev. David Brown, D.D., *A Commentary Critical, Experimental and Practical on the Old and New Testaments* (Grand Rapids: William B. Eerdmans Publishing Co., 1945), vol I., 194.
9. Spurgeon *Sermons* 378.

Chapter Eight: Making Bad Times Good

1. Amy Carmichael, *Kohila* (Fort Washington, Pa.: Christian Literature Crusade, n.d.), 130.
2. Charles H. Spurgeon, *Sermons of Rev. C. H. Spurgeon* (New York: Funk & Wagnalls, 1857), vol. 2, 195.
3. C. S. Lewis, *Letters to an American Lady* (Grand Rapids: William B. Eerdmans Publishing Co., 1971), 110.
4. Rollo May, *Art of Counseling* (Nashville: Abingdon Press, 1967), 162.